WORLD CUP '82
A COMPLETE GUIDE

WORLD CUP '82

A COMPLETE GUIDE

Nicholas Keith and Norman Fox
with photographs by Peter Robinson

PARK LANE PRESS

First published in Great Britain by
Park Lane Press, 40 Park Street, London W1Y 4DE

Text © Nicholas Keith and Norman Fox 1982
© photographs Peter Robinson

ISBN 0 902935 26 7

Designed by Nigel Partridge
Picture research by Tom Graves
Production: Elizabeth Winder
House editor: Erica Hunningher

Text set by SX Composing Limited, Rayleigh, Essex
Printed and bound by Jarrold & Sons Ltd, Norwich

Distributed by Conde Nast & National
Magazine Distributors Ltd (COMAG),
Tavistock Road, West Drayton, Middlesex
UB7 7QE (West Drayton 44055)
Telex 8813787 COMAG C

CONTENTS

HISTORY OF THE WORLD CUP

The 1982 World Cup finals in Spain will be the biggest sporting event of all time. There will be 24 nations competing, more than ever before, and the organizers expect 1,300 million people to tune in their television sets on the evening of 13 June for the opening ceremony followed by the first match in the Nou Camp Stadium, Barcelona. The popularity and success of the World Cup have exceeded the wildest dreams of its French creators, Jules Rimet and Henri Delaunay. The first tournament in 1930 was watched by a total of 434,000 spectators; in 1978, 1.6 million fans watched the tournament in Argentina and the final between Argentina and Holland was seen by 1,000 million on television.

All this was only a twinkle in the eye when the Federation Internationale de Football Associations (FIFA) was formed on 21 May 1904. The idea of a world championship was also born and FIFA took sole rights of organization. This required great foresight because international soccer was in its infancy. After the formation of the English Football Association in 1863, the laws were codified. The gospel of soccer was spread by Britons who were travelling the world in the wake of the industrial revolution. Sailors, students, engineers, businessmen and diplomats introduced the new game wherever they went.

By 1900 the Charnock brothers from Lancashire had introduced soccer into Russia. Charles Miller, whose parents were English and who himself played for Southampton, took the game to Brazil. The English community in Buenos Aires were responsible for its growth in Argentina. English schoolboys and students played the game in Denmark and in the German universities. Hugo Meisl, a great admirer of England, caught the bug in Austria, where English expatriates had first played the game in Vienna. John Dick, a Scot, was the pioneer in Czechoslovakia.

The first international was between England and Scotland; the British championship began in 1883-84. The first international between non-British sides was on 12 October 1902, when Austria beat Hungary 5-0; France and Belgium met for the first time on a soccer pitch only months before FIFA's first meeting. In South America, Sir Thomas Lipton, the tea millionaire, had given a trophy (the Lipton Cup) for international competition. In 1902 it was contested by Argentina and Uruguay. However, nothing daunted the founder nations of FIFA – Belgium, Denmark, France, Holland, Spain, Sweden and Switzerland. At the time three of them had no national association (France, Spain and Sweden) and Denmark, Spain and Switzerland had not played an international.

England, the 'cradle of football', joined FIFA in 1905 and the following year their rules of the game were recognized. But the road to the first World Cup in Uruguay in 1930 was closed completely by the First World War from 1914 to 1918 and littered with disagreements in the 1920s (mainly over the definition of professionalism). After the First World War the British would not play against countries which they had fought or which had remained neutral, and refused to re-join FIFA at first. Differences were settled eventually and the British joined FIFA again in 1924, on good terms for their associations: they were given freedom from interference by FIFA and were exempted from paying a proportion of gate receipts from internationals to the federation.

However, the definition of the amateur was not resolved. The British could not get the other members of FIFA to agree to their strict definition of a professional as anyone who was paid or received 'consideration of any sort above his necessary hotel and travelling expenses actually paid'.

The problem of professionalism was raised again in 1928 when 'broken time' payments were allowed in the Olympic Games in Amsterdam. The British withdrew from the Olympics and from FIFA. They did not return to the fold until 1946 and they were out in the cold when the dream of a World Cup was realized.

Rimet and Delaunay had recognized that the Olympic Games were not a true world championship, because only amateurs were allowed and the professional game was growing. The idea of a World Cup was revived and in 1928 Delaunay and Hugo Meisl were put in charge of the early preparations. They may well have been inspired by the brilliant football of Uruguay, who were Olympic champions in 1924 and 1928 – living proof that soccer had become a world game.

When FIFA met in Barcelona in 1929 it was to decide where the first world championship should be staged. Spain, Holland, Italy and Sweden were the European candidates, but they withdrew leaving the way clear to Uruguay, who in 1930 were celebrating the centenary of the country's independence. Uruguay also promised to pay all teams' travel and hotel expenses and to build a new stadium in Montevideo.

URUGUAY 1930

The generosity of Uruguay did not encourage the Europeans to make the three week trip to South America. Eight weeks before the first World Cup was due to start there were no entries. In the end, France, Belgium and Yugoslavia agreed to play together with Romania (under pressure from King Carol who chose the Romanian team). The South American entrants were Uruguay, Bolivia, Brazil, Chile, Paraguay, Peru and Argentina (who had forced Uruguay to a replay in the 1928 Olympic final).

The field of 13 was completed by Mexico and the United States.

With so few entries, the original plan for a knockout competition was abandoned and the teams were split up into four leagues with a seeded team in each. The pool winners qualified for the semi-finals. The first World Cup game took place on 13 July 1930, when France beat Mexico in Pool One. Argentina were the seeds in this Pool and five goals from Stabile took them into the semi-finals. Brazil were seeded in Pool Two but in their first match they lost to Yugoslavia who beat Bolivia to qualify. Uruguay won Pool Three and the United States justified their seeding with wins over Belgium and Paraguay in Pool Four; with a powerful contingent of British players the Americans were dubbed 'the shot-putters' by the French.

Both semi-finals contained a deluge of second-half goals and finished with the

So happy together: the cup of joy runs over for Castro and Scarone (*right*) as they celebrate Uruguay's victory in the first final against Argentina in Montevideo, 1930.

7

same scoreline, 6-1. The Americans were only 1-0 down to Argentina at half-time but were sunk by three goals in nine minutes, Brown scoring their only goal. Yugoslavia scored first against Uruguay, trailed 2-1 at the interval and crumbled after being denied an equalizer on a controversial offside decision.

Boatloads of Argentines crossed the River Plate from Buenos Aires to Montevideo for the final on 30 July. The crowd was limited to 90,000 although the ground capacity was 100,000. The Belgian referee, John Langenus, demanded guarantees of safety for himself and the linesmen. Pablo Dorado, Uruguay's right wing, scored the first goal in a World Cup final after 12 minutes, but Argentina went ahead through Peucelle and Stabile (his eighth goal of the competition). But second-half goals from Cea, Iriarte and Castro made sure that Uruguay were the first world champions. Later they were to decide not to defend the title.

A national holiday was declared in Uruguay on the day after the final; but in Buenos Aires the Uruguayan consulate was stoned by demonstrators and eventually the two football associations broke off relations. The vivid, violent and passionate story of the World Cup had begun.

POOL ONE

France 4 Mexico 1
Argentina 1 France 0
Chile 3 Mexico 0

Chile 1 France 0
Argentina 6 Mexico 3
Argentina 3 Chile 1

	P	W	D	L	F	A	Pts
Argentina	3	3	0	0	10	4	6
Chile	3	2	0	1	5	3	4
France	3	1	0	2	4	3	2
Mexico	3	0	0	3	4	13	0

POOL TWO

Yugoslavia 2 Brazil 1
Yugoslavia 4 Bolivia 0

Brazil 4 Bolivia 0

	P	W	D	L	F	A	Pts
Yugoslavia	2	2	0	0	6	1	4
Brazil	2	1	0	1	5	2	2
Bolivia	2	0	0	2	0	8	0

POOL THREE

Romania 3 Peru 1
Uruguay 1 Peru 0

Uruguay 4 Romania 0

	P	W	D	L	F	A	Pts
Uruguay	2	2	0	0	5	0	4
Romania	2	1	0	1	3	5	2
Peru	2	0	0	2	1	4	0

POOL FOUR

United States 3 Belgium 0
United States 3 Paraguay 0

Paraguay 1 Belgium 0

	P	W	D	L	F	A	Pts
United States	2	2	0	0	6	0	4
Paraguay	2	1	0	1	1	3	2
Belgium	2	0	0	2	0	4	0

SEMI-FINALS

Argentina 6 United States 1
Uruguay 6 Yugoslavia 1

FINAL (Montevideo, 30 July 1930)

Uruguay (1) 4 Argentina (2) 2

Uruguay: Ballesteros; Nasazzi (capt), Mascheroni, Andrade, Fernandez, Gestido, Dorado, Scarone, Castro, Cea, Iriarte.

Argentina: Botasso; Della Torre, Paternoster, Evaristo J., Monti, Suarez, Peucelle, Varallo, Stabile, Ferreira (capt), Evaristo M.

Scorers: Dorado, Cea, Iriarte, Castro for Uruguay; Peucelle, Stabile for Argentina.

Leading scorer: Stabile (Argentina) 8.

ITALY 1934

Discipline was the keynote of the second World Cup. Two authoritarian Italians dominated the stage: Benito Mussolini, the fascist dictator who needed a home victory to boost his own image, and Vittorio Pozzo, Italy's tough team manager. Of the 32 nations entered, Argentina, Belgium, Brazil, France and the United States were the only survivors from 1930 and there was a qualifying competition to reduce the field to 16.

Uruguay did not attend, the only time the World Cup holders have not defended

Left: we are the champions. The 1930 winning Uruguay team line up, standing (left to right), Gestido, Nasazzi, Ballesteros, Mascheroni, Andrade, Fernandez and Grecco; in front, Dorado, Scarone, Castro, Cea and Iriarte.

Below: half way to paradise: Pozzo (on the left) encourages Italy before extra-time in the 1934 final.

9

their title. Professional football had been recognized only recently in Uruguay and clubs refused to release their players to the national team. Besides, Uruguay were still fuming at Argentina and angry about lack of European interest in 1930.

The first round proper began on 27 May with Italy beating the United States in Rome, 7-1. The Europeans dominated the competition after that and no team from another continent survived the first round. Argentina lost 3-2 to Sweden; they had no survivors from 1930 when they were runners-up, because Italy had reclaimed three of their nationals who had represented Argentina four years before – Guaita, Orsi and Monti (the last named had played in the Montevideo final). Argentina sent a weakened team as a protest and to discourage further poaching of their players.

Spain put out Brazil, 3-1, with all the goals coming in the first half. Germany and Czechoslovakia came from behind to defeat Belgium and Romania. Fancied Austria, who had developed their 'wunderteam' under Hugo Meisl, eliminated France, but only after extra-time. Hungary struggled to a 4-2 victory over Egypt, and Switzerland overcame Holland.

The quarter-finals were spoiled by rough play. Some of the worst of it was at Florence where Italy were held to a 1-1 draw by the brave Spaniards, seven of whom were unfit for the replay, including Zamora, the legendary Spanish goalkeeper. Italy won the replay through a goal by Meazza but the Swiss referee, Mercet, was so inept that he was suspended by his national federation.

There was more bad behaviour at Bologna where Austria beat Hungary 2-1 after the Hungarian right wing, Markos, was sent off in a game which Meisl described as 'a brawl'. In Milan, Germany won 2-1 against Sweden who were down to 10 men in the latter stages of the match; and in Turin the goalkeeping of Planicka for Czechoslovakia denied the strenuous efforts of the Swiss and put his team in the semi-finals.

The semi-final between Italy and Austria in Milan was, on paper, worthy of the final. But both sides were weakened by injury, and a heavy pitch handicapped Austria, who lost to a single goal, scored by Guaita, Italy's Argentine import. Mussolini watched the Czechs overcome Germany in Rome, 3-1. In the play-off for third place in Naples Germany had the ball in the net after 24 seconds and beat Austria, 3-2.

The final in Rome was the first to need extra-time; in fact it was not a sell out with a crowd of 55,000. Czechoslovakia scored first, after 70 minutes through Puc, and they had further chances, but Orsi equalized with a once-in-a-lifetime shot eight minutes from time. Italy's winner fell to Schiavio in the seventh minute of extra-time.

Fanatical support of the home team was a key factor and would be so again. The hosts pocketed the trophy and 1m lire.

FIRST ROUND

Italy 7	United States 1		Spain 3	Brazil 1
Czechoslovakia 2	Romania 1		Switzerland 3	Holland 2
Germany 5	Belgium 2		Sweden 3	Argentina 2
Austria 3	France 2 aet		Hungary 4	Egypt 2

SECOND ROUND

Germany 2	Sweden 1		Italy 1	Spain 1
Austria 2	Hungary 1		*replay*	
Czechoslovakia 3	Switz. 2		Italy 1	Spain 0

SEMI-FINALS

Czechoslovakia 3 Germany 1 (in Rome)
Italy 1 Austria 0 (in Milan)

THIRD PLACE MATCH (Naples)
Germany 3 Austria 2

FINAL (Rome, 10 June 1934)
Italy (0) (1) 2 Czechoslovakia (0) (1) 1 aet

Italy: Combi (capt); Monzeglio, Allemandi, Ferraris IV, Monti, Bertolini, Guaita, Meazza, Schiavio, Ferrari, Orsi.

Czechoslovakia: Planicka (capt); Zenisek, Ctyroky, Kostalek, Cambal, Krcil, Junek, Svoboda, Sobotka, Nejedly, Puc.

Scorers: Orsi, Schiavio for Italy; Puc for Czechoslovakia.

Leading scorers: Schiavio (Italy), Nejedly (Czechoslovakia), Conen (Germany) 4 each.

FRANCE 1938

The third World Cup took place under the menacing clouds of war. German troops had already invaded the Rhineland. Spain was wracked by civil war; Austria qualified but their country was overrun by Germany and they had to withdraw. The continuing agonies over professionalism kept away Uruguay, and Argentina stayed at home because France were preferred as hosts. The 16 qualifiers for the finals, from an entry of 36, included newcomers in Poland, Norway, Cuba and the Dutch East Indies. England refused an invitation to take the place of Austria.

The finals were played on a knockout basis again. In the first round Hungary thrashed the Dutch East Indies and France knocked out Belgium, 3-1. All the other ties needed extra-time or replays. Cuba caused the big upset in a replay against Romania; Switzerland took two matches to get the better of Germany (who included three Austrians). Brazil had a 3-1 half-time lead over Poland, were brought back to 4-4 at the end of 90 minutes and squeezed through 6-5 in the extra period; so did Italy (against Norway) and Czechoslovakia (against Holland).

In the second round the hosts, France, came up against the holders and Italy triumphed, 3-1. Cuba were swamped 8-0 by Sweden, and Switzerland fell to two Hungarian goals by Szengeller. In Bordeaux, two Brazilians (Zeze and Machado) and a Czech (Riha) were sent off. Planicka, the Czech goalkeeper, suffered a broken arm and his colleague, Nejedly, a broken leg; on goals the teams finished 1-1 after extra-time. Brazil won 2-1 in the replay, notable for its improved humour and for 15 changes on the field compared with the first match.

Having brought in nine new faces for the

Too little too late: Sarosi (dark shirt, in the middle) scores Hungary's second goal in the 1938 final but his team were already on their way to a 4-2 defeat by Italy who retained the Jules Rimet trophy.

replay against the Czechs, Brazil now made eight changes for the semi-finals. They even rested Leonidas, their star centre forward, but a penalty put Italy on the way to the final, 2-1. In the other semi-final, Sweden scored after 35 seconds but found themselves 1-4 down and almost out at half-time; the Hungarians completed the formality and Szengeller achieved his hat-trick in the second half.

In the final at the Stade Colombes on 19 June, in front of a crowd of 65,000, Italy retained their crown by cutting out the frills – as their manager Pozzo put it: 'We left aside all flourishes, anything resembling ballet.' Colaussi and Piola shared Italy's goals in a 4-2 victory and Hungary never got closer than 1-1. Brazil took third place, also with a 4-2 victory, over Sweden. The overall tally of goals, 84, was easily the best to date (an average of over 4½ goals a game).

Italy's 'iron man'; Vittorio Pozzo, their manager, holds the World Cup aloft after his team's success against Hungary in the Stade Colombes in Paris, 1938. Now a national hero, Pozzo's team had twice won the World Cup, and the Olympics in 1936.

FIRST ROUND

Switzerland 1 Germany 1 aet	Hungary 6 Dutch E. Indies 0
replay	France 3 Belgium 1 aet
Switzerland 4 Germany 2	Czechoslovakia 3 Holland 0
Cuba 3 Romania 3 aet	Brazil 6 Poland 5
replay	Italy 2 Norway 1
Cuba 2 Rumania 1	Sweden bye

SECOND ROUND

Sweden 8 Cuba 0	Brazil 1 Czechoslovakia 1 aet
Hungary 2 Switzerland 0	*replay*
Italy 3 France 1	Brazil 2 Czechoslovakia 1

SEMI-FINALS

Italy 2   Brazil 1 (in Marseilles)
Hungary 5   Sweden 1 (in Paris)

THIRD PLACE MATCH (Bordeaux)

Brazil 4   Sweden 2

12

FINAL (Paris, 19 June 1938)
Italy (3) 4   Hungary (1) 2

Italy: Olivieri; Foni, Rava; Serantoni, Andreolo, Locatelli; Biavati, Meazza (capt), Piola, Ferrari, Colaussi.

Hungary: Szabo; Polgar, Biro; Szalay, Szucs, Lazar; Sas, Vincze, Sarosi (capt), Szengeller, Titkos.

Scorers: Colaussi 2, Piola 2 for Italy; Titkos, Sarosi for Hungary.

Leading Scorer: Leonidas (Brazil) 8.

BRAZIL 1950

The omens were good for the first World Cup after the Second World War but somehow things turned sour, especially for Brazil, who lost the title to Uruguay in the last match. There were now 73 members of FIFA (an increase of 22 since 1938). The British had re-joined and the Soviet Union had enrolled in the same year, 1946. However, all the Soviet bloc stayed at home; and so did Scotland who qualified by finishing second in the British Championship, but they had said all along that they would go to Brazil only if they were British champions.

Only 13 teams lined up. Portugal refused to take Scotland's place. Argentina were still at loggerheads with Uruguay. Turkey declined their qualifying place and France accepted at first but then changed their mind, mainly because of the travel arrangements offered by the organizers. East and West Germany were excluded by FIFA. On the credit side, gates averaged over 60,000 at each game.

The competition was entirely on a league basis with the winners of four pools going forward to a final pool. This unfortunate system was made worse because the original pools were not regrouped to make allowance for the withdrawals. So there were only two teams in Pool Four and

Left for dead: Italy's hopes of retaining the World Cup in 1950 are buried as Parola (*right*) watches Jeppson of Sweden putting in a cross.

Uruguay just had to beat lowly Bolivia (which they did, 8-0) to reach the Final Pool.

Brazil qualified from Pool One, beating Mexico and Yugoslavia and drawing with Switzerland. Mexico's goalkeeper, Carbajal, played in the first of five World Cup finals. Sweden, the 1948 Olympic champions, emerged as the surprising winners of Pool Three. This team had been rebuilt by George Raynor, its English coach, and it won 3-2 against a disorganized Italy, who had not recovered from the 1949 air crash in which the whole Torino team was killed (including ten internationals).

The big shock of the tournament was in Pool Three, in which England were making their World Cup bow. In their first match, England had a sticky 2-0 victory over Chile in the giant Maracana Stadium in Rio de Janeiro. They travelled to the cooler airs of Belo Horizonte to meet the unrated United States and their team included Alf Ramsey, Billy Wright, Tom Finney and Stan Mortensen (Stanley Matthews was rested). Yet the United States – captained by Eddie McIlvenny who had been given a free transfer from the English third division club Wrexham – triumphed 1-0, the goal scored by Haitian-born Larry Gaetjens after 37 minutes. England had to beat their next opponents, Spain, handsomely in Rio but their forward line (which included Matthews, Milburn and Finney) was bravely denied by Ramallets, the Spanish goalkeeper. Zarra headed the winner for Spain in the second half.

In the Final Pool, Spain began well and led 2-1 at half-time in a rough game against Uruguay through goals by Basora. With Ramallets again in fine form, Uruguay did not equalize until 18 minutes from the end. This effort sapped Spain and they were beaten 6-1 in their next match against Brazil, who had already defeated Sweden, 7-1. The Swedes gained third place with a 3-1 win against Spain.

So, by chance, the last match turned into a Cup Final with Brazil overwhelming favourites to achieve the draw they needed. An estimated 205,000 people crammed into the unfinished Maracana to see them do it on 16 July. For 47 minutes a torrent of Brazilian attacks made no impact on the Uruguay defence, superbly marshalled by Varela and Andrade, with Maspoli performing like an elastic wall in goal. Friaça scored for Brazil in the 47th minute, but Uruguay took the initiative as Varela turned his talents to attack. Goals by Schiaffino and Ghiggia burst Brazil's bubble.

POOL ONE

Brazil 4   Mexico 0

Yugoslavia 3   Switzerland 0

Yugoslavia 4   Mexico 1

Brazil 2   Switzerland 2

Brazil 2   Yugoslavia 0

Switzerland 2   Mexico 1

	P	W	D	L	F	A	Pts
Brazil	3	2	1	0	8	2	5
Yugoslavia	3	2	0	1	7	3	4
Switzerland	3	1	1	1	4	6	3
Mexico	3	0	0	3	2	10	0

POOL TWO

Spain 3   United States 1

England 2   Chile 0

United States 1   England 0

Spain 2   Chile 0

Spain 1   England 0

Chile 5   United States 2

	P	W	D	L	F	A	Pts
Spain	3	3	0	0	6	1	6
England	3	1	0	2	2	2	2
Chile	3	1	0	2	5	6	2
United States	3	1	0	2	4	8	2

POOL THREE

Sweden 3   Italy 2

Sweden 2   Paraguay 2

Italy 2   Paraguay 0

	P	W	D	L	F	A	Pts
Sweden	2	1	1	0	5	4	3
Italy	2	1	0	1	4	3	2
Paraguay	2	0	1	1	2	4	1

POOL FOUR

Uruguay 8   Bolivia 0

	P	W	D	L	F	A	Pts
Uruguay	1	1	0	0	8	0	2
Bolivia	1	0	0	1	0	8	0

FINAL POOL

Final pool replaced knockout system

Uruguay 2   Spain 2

Brazil 7   Sweden 1

Uruguay 3   Sweden 2   Brazil 6   Spain 1
Sweden 3   Spain 1

Uruguay (0) 2   Brazil (0) 1 (Rio de Janeiro, 16 July 1950)

Uruguay: Maspoli; Gonzales, Tejera; Gambetta, Varela (capt), Andrade; Ghiggia, Perez, Miguez, Schiaffino, Moran.

Brazil: Barbosa; Augusto (capt), Juvenal; Bauer, Danilo, Bigode; Friaça, Zizinho, Ademir, Jair, Chico.

Scorers: Schiaffino, Ghiggia for Uruguay; Friaça for Brazil.

	P	W	D	L	F	A	Pts
Uruguay	3	2	1	0	7	5	5
Brazil	3	2	0	1	14	4	4
Sweden	3	1	0	2	6	11	2
Spain	3	0	1	2	4	11	1

Leading scorer: Ademir (Brazil) 7.

SWITZERLAND 1954

The fifth World Cup was expected to be a Hungarian rhapsody. Olympic champions in 1952, Hungary had developed into one of the most brilliant national teams of all time with great players such as Grosics, the goalkeeper, Bozsik, the dynamic wing-half, Puskas, with his lethal left foot, and Hidegkuti, the revolutionary deep-lying centre forward.

These finals were also the first to be televised and there was yet another new format with the 16 finalists divided into four groups and the first two in each group entering a knockout competition. As a twist, two teams in each group were seeded and seeds were not to meet until the quarter-finals. So play-offs were inevitable.

West Germany, who were back in the international fold but were unseeded, were in Group Two with Hungary, Turkey and Korea. They beat Turkey and virtually conceded their game against Hungary (knowing that they would have only to beat Turkey again in a play-off to reach the last eight). Hungary won 8-3 with Kocsis scoring four but they lost Puskas who injured

an ankle and did not play again until the final. Hungary qualified with ease having already smashed Korea, 9-0. West Germany duly won their play-off against Turkey, 7-2.

Brazil and Yugoslavia went through from Group One with France and Mexico eliminated. In Group Three, Scotland made their first World Cup appearance and their manager, Andy Beattie, resigned because of criticism when they lost their first match 1-0 against Austria. So it was hardly surprising that Scotland then crashed 7-0 to Uruguay, the only other South American team. In Group Four, England progressed to the quarter-finals after a 4-4 draw against Belgium and a 2-0 win over Switzerland who put out the seeded Italians in a play-off.

There were 18 goals in the first two quarter-finals. Matthews had a splendid match for England against Uruguay but

Scotland the brave: Martin, the Scottish goalkeeper, keeps everything crossed as he rebuffs a Uruguay attack in Basle in 1954. Seven Uruguayan goals got past him.

could not prevent the holders from winning, 4-2. England's goals were scored by Lofthouse and Finney but poor goalkeeping by Merrick let in the Uruguayans. On the same day, 26 June, Austria came back from 0-3 down after 20 minutes to lead 5-4 at half time and emerge as 7-5 victors over Switzerland in the World Cup's highest scoring match.

The next day West Germany beat Yugoslavia 2-0 to earn a semi-final match against Austria. The least said about the fourth quarter-final the better. Hungary's 4-2 win against Brazil is better known as the 'Battle of Berne' with two penalties and three players (Nilton Santos and Tozzi, of Brazil, and Bozsik, of Hungary) sent off by the English referee, Arthur Ellis. The battle was resumed in the dressing rooms afterwards, but neither Hungary nor Brazil would discipline their players.

The semi-final between Uruguay and Hungary in Lausanne helped to restore the good name of football. Uruguay fought back from two goals down to force extra-time, but two goals from Kocsis sealed the match for Hungary. In the other semi-final in Basle, West Germany put five goals past Austria in the second half to win 6-1.

Hungary restored Puskas for the final on 14 July although he was not fit. Surprisingly, they preferred Toth to the talented Budai on the wing and, to make room for him, Czibor moved from the left to the right flank. They were two goals up in eight minutes through Puskas and Czibor, but the determined Germans had equalized within 10 minutes, Morlock and Rahn getting the goals. In the second half the Hungarians were denied by the bar, a post and Turek, the German goalkeeper. Five minutes from the end Rahn scored Germany's winner, although Puskas had the ball in the net again only to be ruled offside.

Left: at full stretch: Parlier the Swiss goalkeeper (on the left) and his defence have an anxious time against Italy in the qualifying rounds in 1954. Switzerland won the match 2-1 and had to beat Italy in a play-off to go through to the quarter-finals, where they were eliminated 7-5 by Austria.

Right: the 'Battle of Berne': Brazil's Didi is challenged by Hungary's Lantos during the infamous 1954 quarter-final. The fighting continued in the dressing rooms.

GROUP ONE

Yugoslavia 1   France 0
Brazil 5   Mexico 0

France 3   Mexico 2
Brazil 1   Yugoslavia 1 aet

	P	W	D	L	F	A	Pts
Brazil	2	1	1	0	6	1	3
Yugoslavia	2	1	1	0	2	1	3
France	2	1	0	1	3	3	2
Mexico	2	0	0	2	2	8	0

GROUP TWO

Hungary 9   Korea 0
W. Germany 4   Turkey 1

Hungary 8   W. Germany 3
Turkey 7   Korea 0

	P	W	D	L	F	A	Pts
Hungary	2	2	0	0	17	3	4
West Germany	2	1	0	1	7	9	2
Turkey	2	1	0	1	8	4	2
Korea	2	0	0	2	0	16	0

Play-off: West Germany 7   Turkey 2

GROUP THREE

Austria 1   Scotland 0
Uruguay 2   Czechoslovakia 0

Austria 5   Czechoslovakia 0
Uruguay 7   Scotland 0

	P	W	D	L	F	A	Pts
Uruguay	2	2	0	0	9	0	4
Austria	2	2	0	0	6	0	4
Czechoslovakia	2	0	0	2	0	7	0
Scotland	2	0	0	2	0	8	0

GROUP FOUR

England 4   Belgium 4 aet
England 2   Switzerland 0

Switzerland 2   Italy 1
Italy 4   Belgium 1

	P	W	D	L	F	A	Pts
England	2	1	1	0	6	4	3
Italy	2	1	0	1	5	3	2
Switzerland	2	1	0	1	2	3	2
Belgium	2	0	1	1	5	8	1

Play-off: Switzerland 4   Italy 1

QUARTER-FINALS

W. Germany 2   Yugoslavia 0
Hungary 4   Brazil 2
Austria 7   Switzerland 5
Uruguay 4   England 2

Hungary's attacking line-up

Before the 1950s tactics had changed gradually. One of the first 'tactics' at the beginning of this century was a defensive ploy – the 'offside trap'. In those days a player was offside if there were fewer than three opponents between him and the defending goal. Defenders soon learned that by moving forward they could catch opponents offside. This led to a goal famine and in 1925 the offside law was changed. Now a player was onside if only two opponents were between him and the goal.

Goals abounded and in the 1930s Herbert Chapman's Arsenal withdrew the centre-half from his original midfield role. This was the classic W-M formation which lasted until the 1950s. W in attack, with the two inside forwards playing behind the centre-forward and two wingers. M in defence, with the full-backs and centre-half at the rear and the wing-halves linking in midfield.

The Hungarians withdrew their centre-forward to a deep-lying position. The centre-half was pulled out of place if he marked the Hungarian centre-forward, Hidegkuti. This left room for the goalscoring inside forwards, Puskas and Kocsis. If unmarked, Hidegkuti could sneak into attacking positions and score.

Other key figures in this line-up were Bozsik, the right-half, and the wingers Czibor and Budai or Toth.

Switzerland 1954 (continued)

SEMI-FINALS
W. Germany 6   Austria 1 (in Basle)
Hungary 4   Uruguay 2 (in Lausanne)

THIRD PLACE MATCH (Zurich)
Austria 3   Uruguay 1

FINAL (Berne, 4 July 1954)
W. Germany (2) 3   Hungary (2) 2

West Germany: Turek; Posipal, Kohlmeyer; Eckel, Liebrich, Mai; Rahn, Morlock, Walter O., Walter F. (capt), Schaefer.

Hungary: Grosics; Buzansky, Lantos; Bozsik, Lorant, Zakarias; Czibor, Kocsis, Hidegkuti, Puskas (capt), Toth J.

Scorers: Morlock, Rahn 2 for West Germany; Puskas, Czibor for Hungary.

Leading scorer: Kocsis (Hungary) 11.

For king and country: the Swedish team are presented to King Gustav Adolf at the Stolna Stadium, Stockholm, before they play their first match, against Mexico, in the 1958 finals. The king was pleased with a 3-0 win.

SWEDEN 1958

Brazil scaled the summit at last with the precocious Pelé scoring two goals in the final at the age of 17. Russia competed for the first time and reached the last eight. The four British teams qualified together for the finals for the first time. Television and commercialism came of age and these were the first modern finals.

These are the bare bones of the sixth World Cup, which did not live up to expectation although Just Fontaine, of France, scored a record number of goals, 13. Brazil's success was founded equally on the organization of their coach, Vicente Feola, and on the incredible skills of Pelé and Garrincha, the 'little bird'. But they were not at their best until the semi-final and final.

West Germany headed Group One, even

The 'little bird' swoops: Garrincha centres from the right for Vavà (20) to score the first goal in the 1958 final against Sweden. The 17-year-old Pelé is right there and he went on to score two goals in the second half in Brazil's 5-2 victory. Pelé's genius was to dominate for the next 12 years.

though they had lost seven of the winning side of 1954. Northern Ireland achieved a place in the quarter-finals after winning a play-off against Czechoslovakia, 2-1 after extra-time with McParland getting their goals. The Czech Bubernik was sent off. In Group Four, England drew all their matches – against Russia, Brazil and Austria – but they went down 1-0 to the Soviet Union in a play-off. England were unlucky because Brabrook, a new cap, twice hit a post. They were also deprived of Manchester United stars such as Duncan Edwards, Tommy Taylor and Roger Byrne who had been killed in the Munich air disaster. But they had only themselves to blame for leaving behind Matthews and Lofthouse and for not giving Bobby Charlton a game. Brazil eased through although they did not

play Pelé or Garrincha until their last group game against the Soviet Union. The Brazilian players insisted that Garrincha should be given a game.

Scotland finished bottom of Group Two with one point from a 1-1 draw against Yugoslavia, who qualified with France. In Group Three, Wales matched Northern Ireland exactly. They beat Hungary 2-1 in extra-time of a play-off to clinch their place in the last eight; Ivor Allchurch and Terry Medwin scored the goals.

In the quarter-finals Wales were without their star player John Charles, but they fought magnificently in losing 1-0 to Brazil; Pelé's winning goal was deflected by a Welsh defender. Northern Ireland damaged their chances by making a long coach trip the day before their game against France. They crashed 4-0, with three goals coming in the second half. Still, the Irish had enjoyed their finest hour in international football under the guidance of Peter Doherty, their manager, and with

Brazil's 4-2-4 system

The winning formula: the diagram shows the 4-2-4 formation which Brazil used in 1958. The creative midfield players Didi and Zito provided the bullets for Vavà and Pelé to fire the goals. Garrincha ran defences ragged on the right and Zagalo mopped up on the left in defence and attack. The Brazilian team: (back row, left to right) D. Santos, Zito, Bellini, N. Santos, Orlando and Gilmar; (front) Garrincha, Didi, Pelé, Vavà and Zagalo.

the form of players such as Danny Blanchflower, Jimmy McIlroy and Billy Bingham (who is now their manager).

Rahn, the German hero in the 1954 final, scored the only goal of the match against Yugoslavia, and Swedish pressure told in the end against Russia, the hosts winning 2-0. In the semi-finals, Fontaine became the first to score against Brazil but injury-hit France crashed 5-2. The other tie was notable for the fervour of the Swedish fans who had not shown much interest before but supported their team fanatically in a 3-1 victory over West Germany. Fontaine scored four times in France's 6-3 win against West Germany in the play-off for third place. In the final, Sweden scored in the first minute. But instead of cracking, as George Raynor, the Swedish manager, had predicted, Brazil stayed cool and Pelé scored twice in a thrilling 5-2 victory.

GROUP ONE
W. Germany 3 Argentina 1
N. Ireland 1 Czechoslovakia 0
W. Germany 2 Czechoslovakia 2
Argentina 3 N. Ireland 1
W. Germany 2 N. Ireland 2
Czechoslovakia 6 Argentina 1

	P	W	D	L	F	A	Pts
West Germany	3	1	2	0	7	5	4
Czechoslovakia	3	1	1	1	8	4	3
Northern Ireland	3	1	1	1	4	5	3
Argentina	3	1	0	2	5	10	2

Play-off: Northern Ireland 2 Czechoslovakia 1 aet

GROUP TWO
France 7 Paraguay 3
Yugoslavia 1 Scotland 1
Yugoslavia 3 France 2

Paraguay 3 Scotland 2
France 2 Scotland 1
Yugoslavia 3 Paraguay 3

	P	W	D	L	F	A	Pts
France	3	2	0	1	11	7	4
Yugoslavia	3	1	2	0	7	6	4
Paraguay	3	1	1	1	9	12	3
Scotland	3	0	1	2	4	6	1

GROUP THREE
Sweden 3 Mexico 0
Hungary 1 Wales 1
Wales 1 Mexico 1

Sweden 2 Hungary 1
Sweden 0 Wales 0
Hungary 4 Mexico 0

	P	W	D	L	F	A	Pts
Sweden	3	2	1	0	5	1	5
Hungary	3	1	1	1	6	3	3
Wales	3	0	3	0	2	2	3
Mexico	3	0	1	2	1	8	1

Play-off: Wales 2 Hungary 1

GROUP FOUR
England 2 USSR 2
Brazil 3 Austria 0
England 0 Brazil 0

USSR 2 Austria 0
Brazil 2 USSR 0
England 2 Austria 2

	P	W	D	L	F	A	Pts
Brazil	3	2	1	0	5	0	5
England	3	0	3	0	4	4	3
USSR	3	1	1	1	4	4	3
Austria	3	0	1	2	2	7	1

Play-off: USSR 1 England 0

QUARTER-FINALS
France 4 N. Ireland 0
W. Germany 1 Yugoslavia 0
Sweden 2 USSR 0
Brazil 1 Wales 0

SEMI-FINALS
Brazil 5 France 2 (in Stockholm)
Sweden 3 W. Germany 1 (in Gothenburg)

THIRD PLACE MATCH (Gothenburg)
France 6 W. Germany 3

FINAL (Stockholm, 29 June 1958)
Brazil (2) 5 Sweden (1) 2

Brazil: Gilmar; Santos D., Santos N.; Zito, Bellini, Orlando, Garrincha, Didi, Vavà, Pelé, Zagalo.

Sweden: Svensson; Bergmark, Axbom; Boerjesson, Gustavsson, Parliag, Hamrin, Gren, Simonsson, Liedholm, Skoglund.

Scorers: Vavà 2, Pelé 2, Zagalo for Brazil; Liedholm, Simonsson for Sweden.

Leading scorer: Fontaine (France) 13 (present record total).

CHILE 1962

The seventh World Cup produced a competition almost as poor as the country which staged it, although Chile had made tremendous and successful efforts to build new stadiums and provide the right set-

The strong arm of the law: Italy's Salvadore is restrained by police during the violent game between Chile and Italy in the 1962 finals. Chile the hosts won 2-0 after complaints about Italy's imported players.

ting. Unfortunately, defences dominated and there were only 89 goals, compared with 126 in 1958 and 140 in 1954.

In Group One, Russia and Yugoslavia qualified at the expense of Uruguay and Columbia, but not before they had been involved in a tough match in which Dubinski, of Russia, had a leg broken and Mujic, the culprit, was sent home.

In Group Two, there was an even more violent game between Chile and Italy. Two Italians, Ferrini and David, were sent off and the Chilean Sanchez should have been when he broke Maschio's nose but referee Ken Aston was unsighted. There was bad blood from the start because the Italians had players in their team who were not their own nationals but had been pillaged

from South America. The Chileans for their part were furious because of hostile articles about their country in the Italian press. Chile beat the nine men of Italy, 2-0, and progressed to the quarter-finals, although they lost their last game against West Germany, the other qualifiers.

In Group Three, Brazil struggled to find form, beating Mexico 2-0 and being held to a goalless draw by the Czechs. A pulled muscle in this game also cost them the services of Pelé for the rest of the tournament. However, Garrincha came into his own and they found an excellent replacement for Pelé in the teenager Amarildo. Spain were also in this group under the managership of Helenio Herrera, once manager of Inter Milan. Their squad included the brilliant Suarez, Santamaria (once of Uruguay), di Stefano and Puskas, the Hungarian master. But di Stefano was never fit to play, their only result was a 1-0 win against Mexico and the Czechs went forward with Brazil. England, the only British representatives, qualified from Group Four with Hungary who had raised their hopes with a 6-1 thrashing of Bulgaria, but surprisingly went down 1-0 to Czechoslovakia in the quarter-finals.

In the other quarter-finals, England could find no answer to Garrincha at Viña del Mar. He scored the first goal, made the second for Vavà and hit a swerving free-kick for the third of Brazil's goals; Hitchens had notched a first-half equalizer for England. In Arica in the far north, Yachin, the mighty Russian goalkeeper, proved fallible and let in Chile for a 2-1 win, while in Santiago Yugoslavia gained a long-awaited World Cup success against West Germany.

In the semi-finals, Brazil were far too good for Chile, although the hosts went on to take third place. Yugoslavia had much of the play in front of only 5,000 spectators in Viña del Mar; but the canny Czechs'

patient tactics worked and they won 3-1. However, in the final Czechoslovakia were let down by their goalkeeper, Schroiff, who had been superb until then. Masopust put Czechoslovakia ahead after 16 minutes but Brazil equalized through Amarildo and retained the trophy with second-half goals from Zito and Vavà.

GROUP ONE

Uruguay 2 Colombia 1			USSR 4 Colombia 4		
USSR 2 Yugoslavia 0			USSR 2 Uruguay 1		
Yugoslavia 3 Uruguay 1			Yugoslavia 5 Colombia 0		

	P	W	D	L	F	A	Pts
USSR	3	2	1	0	8	5	5
Yugoslavia	3	2	0	1	8	3	4
Uruguay	3	1	0	2	4	6	2
Colombia	3	0	1	2	5	11	1

The understudy stars: Amarildo, who replaced the injured Pelé in the 1962 finals, is embraced during Brazil's 2-1 win over Spain in Viña del Mar. Spain had led 1-0 at half-time but late in the second half Garrincha laid on two goals for Amarildo.

GROUP TWO

Chile 3	Switzerland 1		W. Germany 2	Switzerland 1			
W. Germany 0	Italy 0		W. Germany 2	Chile 0			
Chile 2	Italy 0		Italy 3	Switzerland 0			

	P	W	D	L	F	A	Pts
West Germany	3	2	1	0	4	1	5
Chile	3	2	0	1	5	3	4
Italy	3	1	1	1	3	2	3
Switzerland	3	0	0	3	2	8	0

GROUP THREE

Brazil 2	Mexico 0		Spain 1	Mexico 0	
Czechoslovakia 1	Spain 0		Brazil 2	Spain 1	
Brazil 0	Czechoslovakia 0		Mexico 3	Czechoslovakia 1	

	P	W	D	L	F	A	Pts
Brazil	3	2	1	0	4	1	5
Czechoslovakia	3	1	1	1	2	3	3
Mexico	3	1	0	2	3	4	2
Spain	3	1	0	2	2	3	2

GROUP FOUR

Argentina 1	Bulgaria 0		Hungary 6	Bulgaria 1	
Hungary 2	England 1		Argentina 0	Hungary 0	
England 3	Argentina 1		England 0	Bulgaria 0	

	P	W	D	L	F	A	Pts
Hungary	3	2	1	0	8	2	5
England	3	1	1	1	4	3	3
Argentina	3	1	1	1	2	3	3
Bulgaria	3	0	1	2	1	7	1

QUARTER-FINALS
Yugoslavia 1   W. Germany 0
Brazil 3   England 1
Chile 2   USSR 1
Czechoslovakia 1   Hungary 0

SEMI-FINALS
Brazil 4   Chile 2 (in Santiago)
Czechoslovakia 3   Yugoslavia 1 (in Viña del Mar)

THIRD PLACE MATCH (Santiago)
Chile 1   Yugoslavia 0

FINAL (Santiago, 17 June 1962)
Brazil (1) 3   Czechoslovakia (1) 1

Brazil: Gilmar; Santos D., Mauro, Zozimo, Santos N.; Zito, Didi; Garrincha, Vavà, Amarildo, Zagalo.

Czechoslovakia: Schroiff; Tichy, Novak; Pluskal, Popluhar, Masopust, Pospichal, Scherer, Kvasniak, Kadraba, Jelinek.

Scorers: Amarildo, Zito, Vavà for Brazil; Masopust for Czechoslovakia.

Leading scorer: Jerkovic (Yugoslavia) 5.

ENGLAND 1966

England had their finest hour and became the first host nation to win the World Cup since Italy in 1934; like Italy they had to go to extra-time in the final. As in Chile, defences dominated and the total goal tally was the same as in 1962.

Alf Ramsey was the undisputed architect of England's success. He ignored all the jibes about his 'wingless wonders' to fashion a balanced team based on the class of Banks in goal, Moore in defence and Bobby Charlton in attack; the spirit of Stiles and Ball; on the versatility of the overlapping full backs, Cohen and Wilson. There was also the elusiveness of Peters (once described by Ramsey as 'ten years ahead of his time') and the dramatic goal-

Human pyramid: Italy can find no answers to the mysteries of the North Korean defence as they are put out of the 1966 World Cup at Goodison Park, Liverpool.

25

scoring of Hurst, who became the first man to get a hat-trick in the final.

This World Cup was also memorable for the stirring deeds of North Korea in Group Four. They began by losing 3-0 to Russia at Middlesbrough and drawing 1-1 with Chile. Next they achieved a sensational upset by beating Italy 1-0, with a goal after 42 minutes by Pak Doo Ik. Italy, who had also lost by the same score to Russia, were out and the North Koreans joined the Soviets in the last eight.

England had qualified for the quarter-finals from Group One after a tedious 0-0 draw against Uruguay in the first match at Wembley and 2-0 wins over both Mexico and France. Jimmy Greaves, the main English goalscorer, was injured against France and this let Hurst into the side. Uruguay also went through with a win over France and another goalless draw against Mexico.

In Group Three, Brazil's experienced side was well beaten in its second game by Hungary, who had lost their first game to

A thin red line: Cohen (2) and Jackie Charlton look back in anguish as Seeler and Emmerich close in on the England goalmouth during the final at Wembley in 1966.

Portugal. Pelé was unfit and Albert, in Hidegkuti's deep-lying role, commanded the stage in Hungary's fine 3-1 win. It was Brazil's first defeat in the finals since 1954. For their last game Brazil brought back a half-fit Pelé, who was promptly kicked off the pitch by the uncompromising Portuguese. Brazil were beaten 3-1 again, and Portugal and Hungary advanced.

In Group Two, West Germany started well, beating the Swiss 5-0, but they were held 0-0 by Argentina and overcame Spain only 2-1 with a goal by Seeler six minutes from the end. Argentina earned a quarter-final place against England by defeating Spain 2-1 and Switzerland 2-0.

In the quarter-finals, Argentina incensed the English – and Alf Ramsey in particular – with their tough and petulant play. Eventually Rattin, the Argentine captain, was sent off nine minutes from the interval and his colleagues threatened to walk off with him. Hurst's second-half goal was enough, although Argentina's 10 men gave England plenty to worry about. The bad feeling after the match remained for years.

The best and brightest of the quarter-finals was between North Korea and Portugal at Goodison Park in Liverpool. The popular Koreans delighted everyone except their opponents by taking a 3-0 lead within 24 minutes. But Eusebio scored four times and Augusto a fifth to restore sanity. West Germany ran out easy 4-0 winners against Uruguay at Hillsborough, Sheffield, with two South Americans (Troche and Silva) sent off by referee Jim Finney. Russia proved too strong for Hungary at Sunderland.

In the semi-finals, West Germany beat nine fit Russians (Sabo was injured early in the match and Chislenko sent off). England won by the same score against Portugal, 2-1, with Stiles blotting out Eusebio, the leading scorer in the tournament. Bobby Charlton scored twice and Eusebio replied from the penalty spot.

In the final, West Germany silenced the Wembley crowd with a goal by Haller after 13 minutes following a mistake by Wilson. Hurst levelled the scores from a Moore free-kick and in the second half Peters gave England the lead. Then England had to suffer the agony of an equalizing goal by Weber in the last 60 seconds.

In the tenth minute of extra-time Ball beat Schnellinger on the right wing and centred to Hurst whose shot hit the under-side of the crossbar and bounced down in the goalmouth. Dienst, the referee, was not sure whether the ball had crossed the line but Bakhramov, the Russian linesman, raised his flag to signal a goal and after a consultation the score was allowed to stand. In the final minutes of extra-time, with the Germans seeking another equalizer, Hurst was put away on the left and let fly with his left foot (hoping that at least the ball would travel far into the stand and gain vital seconds for England). The shot flew unerringly into the roof of the net, the final whistle blew and England, the father

of football, had won 4-2.

The whole nation rose in one triumphant body: 100,000 fans at Wembley and millions more watching at home on television.

GROUP ONE

England 0	Uruguay 0	England 2	Mexico 0
France 1	Mexico 1	Uruguay 0	Mexico 0
Uruguay 2	France 1	England 2	France 0

	P	W	D	L	F	A	Pts
England	3	2	1	0	4	0	5
Uruguay	3	1	2	0	2	1	4
Mexico	3	0	2	1	1	3	2
France	3	0	1	2	2	5	1

GROUP TWO

W. Germany 5	Switzerland 0	Argentina 0	W. Germany 0
Argentina 2	Spain 1	Argentina 2	Switzerland 0
Spain 2	Switzerland 1	W. Germany 2	Spain 1

	P	W	D	L	F	A	Pts
West Germany	3	2	1	0	7	1	5
Argentina	3	2	1	0	4	1	5
Spain	3	1	0	2	4	5	2
Switzerland	3	0	0	3	1	9	0

GROUP THREE

Brazil 2	Bulgaria 0	Portugal 3	Bulgaria 0
Portugal 3	Hungary 1	Portugal 3	Brazil 1
Hungary 3	Brazil 1	Hungary 3	Bulgaria 1

	P	W	D	L	F	A	Pts
Portugal	3	3	0	0	9	2	6
Hungary	3	2	0	1	7	5	4
Brazil	3	1	0	2	4	6	2
Bulgaria	3	0	0	3	1	8	0

GROUP FOUR

USSR 3	North Korea 0	USSR 1	Italy 0
Italy 2	Chile 0	North Korea 1	Italy 0
Chile 1	North Korea 1	USSR 2	Chile 1

	P	W	D	L	F	A	Pts
USSR	3	3	0	0	6	1	6
North Korea	3	1	1	1	2	4	3
Italy	3	1	0	2	2	2	2
Chile	3	0	1	2	2	5	1

QUARTER-FINALS

England 1 Argentina 0
W. Germany 4 Uruguay 0
Portugal 5 North Korea 3
USSR 2 Hungary 1

SEMI-FINALS
W. Germany 2   USSR 1 (at Goodison Park)
England 2   Portugal 1 (at Wembley)

THIRD PLACE MATCH (Wembley)
Portugal 2   USSR 1

FINAL (Wembley, 30 July 1966)
England (1) (2) 4   W. Germany (1) (2) 2 aet

England: Banks; Cohen, Wilson; Stiles, Charlton J., Moore; Ball, Hurst, Hunt, Charlton R., Peters.

West Germany: Tilkowski; Hottges, Schulz, Weber, Schnellinger; Haller, Beckenbauer; Overath, Seeler, Held, Emmerich.

Scorers: Hurst 3, Peters for England; Haller, Weber for West Germany.

Leading scorer: Eusebio (Portugal) 9.

MEXICO 1970

Mexico was a controversial choice. Many people thought that the country's climate (intense heat and high altitude) would be a recipe for bad football; that it would lead to violence and negative play. The omens were not good when a qualifying match between El Salvador and Honduras sparked off a war between the two countries. But the dust settled, El Salvador took their place and Brazil emerged triumphant from a competition that was full of good soccer. As this was Brazil's third success they kept the Jules Rimet trophy permanently.

In deference to television the finals began at noon on Sunday 31 May with a scoreless draw between Mexico and Russia in the Aztec Stadium in Group One. Both qualified for the last eight from this group with comfortable victories over Belgium and El Salvador. Italy won Group Two, although they scored only one goal, against Sweden in their first match. In fact there were a mere six goals in all in this tight group and Uruguay pipped Sweden on goal difference, with Israel last.

England and Brazil had been drawn together in Group Three with Romania and Czechoslovakia. Brazil, managed by

Zagalo, who had played for them on the wing in 1958 and 1962, gained maximum points. Their hardest match was at Guadalajara against England in front of a capacity 75,000 crowd. Jairzinho scored the winning goal although England would not have been flattered by a draw and Banks made the save of the tournament from a Pelé header. England qualified with 1-0 wins over Romania and Czechoslovakia.

In Group Four, West Germany scored a hatful of goals. They began shakily against Morocco who took the lead, but goals by Seeler and Müller gave them victory. Müller had a hat-trick in Germany's next match, a 5-2 romp against Bulgaria, and he repeated the feat in his side's 3-1 win over Peru. This did not prevent Peru from booking a berth in the last eight against Brazil.

In this quarter-final encounter at Guadalajara, Peru went down 4-2 to Brazil in their cheerfully attacking manner and Cubillas scored his fifth goal of the series for them. England travelled to Leon for a repeat of the 1966 final against West Germany and they led 2-0 midway through the second half. But Sir Alf Ramsey (as he now was) made the fatal error of changing a winning team in the middle of the game, substituting Hunter and Bell for Peters and Charlton. The Germans drew level with goals in the 70th and 82nd minutes, and Müller forced in the winner in extra-time.

It was in the 27th minute of extra-time that Uruguay scored the goal which put paid to Russia in Mexico City. Italy beat Mexico 4-1 but were not particularly impressive. However, their semi-final against West Germany in the Aztec Stadium proved to be a thriller. A ninth-minute goal by Boninsegna almost saw Italy through without having to play extra-time, but fierce second-half pressure by West Germany was rewarded by an equalizer

The master in attack: Pelé takes on the Italians during Brazil's brilliant display in the 1970 finals in Mexico City. Italy had brief hopes of glory when they levelled the scores at 1-1 but Brazil turned on the heat and ran out comfortable 4-1 winners.

from Schnellinger in the second minute of injury time. Then came the fireworks. There were three goals in the first period of extra-time: Müller gave West Germany the lead, Burgnich levelled the match and Riva put Italy in front again. Naturally it was Müller who equalized with his tenth goal of the tournament, but straight from the kick-off Boninsegna gave Rivera the opportunity to grab the winner.

In the other semi-final, Brazil and Uruguay met for the first time in a World Cup since 1950. Uruguay scored first and held on until just before the interval when Clodoaldo restored the balance. Brazil came good in the second half and further efforts from Jairzinho and Rivelino put them in their fourth final.

West Germany's 1-0 win against Uruguay in a skilful play-off for third place was a suitable curtain-raiser for Brazil's masterly display in the final. Their beautiful 4-1 victory was a triumph for football as much as a defeat for Italy. Jairzinho scored one of the goals to become the first player to be on target in every game in a final. Pelé, Gerson and Carlos Alberto were Brazil's other scorers against a lone goal by Boninsegna, which had given Italy a first-half equalizer and raised their hopes that they might frustrate their talented opponents.

GROUP A
Mexico 0 USSR 0	Mexico 4 El Salvador 0
Belgium 3 El Salvador 0	USSR 2 El Salvador 0
USSR 4 Belgium 1	Belgium 0 Mexico 1

	P	W	D	L	F	A	Pts
USSR	3	2	1	0	6	1	5
Mexico	3	2	1	0	5	0	5
Belgium	3	1	0	2	4	5	2
El Salvador	3	0	0	3	0	9	0

GROUP B
Uruguay 2 Israel 0	Israel 1 Sweden 1
Italy 1 Sweden 0	Sweden 1 Uruguay 0
Uruguay 0 Italy 0	Israel 0 Italy 0

	P	W	D	L	F	A	Pts
Italy	3	1	2	0	1	0	4
Uruguay	3	1	1	1	2	1	3
Sweden	3	1	1	1	2	2	3
Israel	3	0	2	1	1	3	2

GROUP C
England 1 Romania 0	Brazil 1 England 0
Brazil 4 Czechoslovakia 1	Brazil 3 Romania 2
Romania 2 Czechoslovakia 1	England 1 Czechoslovakia 0

	P	W	D	L	F	A	Pts
Brazil	3	3	0	0	8	3	6
England	3	2	0	1	2	1	4
Romania	3	1	0	2	4	5	2
Czechoslovakia	3	0	0	3	2	7	0

GROUP D
Peru 3 Bulgaria 2	W. Germany 5 Bulgaria 2
W. Germany 2 Morocco 0	W. Germany 3 Peru 1
Peru 3 Morocco 0	Bulgaria 1 Morocco 1

	P	W	D	L	F	A	Pts
West Germany	3	3	0	0	10	4	6
Peru	3	2	0	1	7	5	4
Bulgaria	3	0	1	2	5	9	1
Morocco	3	0	1	2	2	6	1

QUARTER-FINALS
Uruguay 1 USSR 0
Italy 4 Mexico 1
Brazil 4 Peru 2
W. Germany 3 England 2 aet

SEMI-FINALS
Italy 4 W. Germany 3 aet (in Mexico City)
Brazil 3 Uruguay 1 (in Guadalajara)

THIRD PLACE MATCH (Mexico City)
W. Germany 1 Uruguay 0

FINAL (Mexico City, 21 June 1970)
Brazil (1) 4 Italy (1) 1

Brazil: Felix; Carlos Alberto, Brito, Piazza, Everaldo, Gerson, Clodoaldo; Jairzinho, Pelé, Tostâo, Rivelino.

Italy: Albertosi; Burgnich, Cera, Rosato, Fachetti; Bertini (Juliano), Riva; Domenghini, Mazzola, De Sisti, Boninsegna (Rivera).

Scorers: Pelé, Gerson, Jairzinho, Carlos Alberto for Brazil; Boninsegna for Italy.

Leading scorer: Müller (West Germany) 10.

WEST GERMANY 1974

A new trophy and a new format were devised for the tenth World Cup. Pelé had retired but Johan Cruyff and Holland's 'total football' had arrived. West Germany carried off the new FIFA World Cup with only one defeat blotting their copybook – at the hands of East Germany.

Controversy and confusion had abounded in the pre-qualifying competition which had begun in 1971 with 95 entries and 23 preliminary groups. As teams from the continents of North America, Africa and Asia were allotted a berth among the final 16, Europe and South America were not given all the places the strength of their football demanded. So Chile and Russia had to play off, home and away. After a goalless draw in Moscow, the Russians refused to play in Chile because the stadium in Santiago had been used as a prison camp. Chile went to West Germany by default. In Africa, Morocco would not play a return game against Zaire who went on to qualify. In Europe, England were eliminated in their qualifying group by Poland, who continued to improve and finished in third place. Italy were held to a 0-0 draw in Naples by Turkey but they remained unbeaten and when the finals began had not conceded a goal for 12 internationals.

Among the hard luck stories in the pre-qualifying competition, the cruellest belonged to Belgium who were unbeaten but pipped for a place by Holland's superior goal difference; Spain lost to Yugoslavia in a play-off and Trinidad had four goals disallowed in their match with Haiti who qualified by winning 2-1.

Brazil kicked off the tournament with a goalless draw against Yugoslavia in Group Two, which also included Zaire and Scotland, who had become the only British contenders by putting out Czechoslovakia. The new format meant that the top two teams in each of the four groups would advance to two new groups and the winners of these leagues would meet for the title (the runners-up competing for third place).

Scotland could put only two goals past Zaire in their first match and then met Brazil in Frankfurt. They achieved a brave 0-0 draw, with Billy Bremner, their 32-year-old captain, in outstanding form. But Yugoslavia hammered Zaire 9-0 to equal the record in the finals and the Scots needed to beat the Slavs in their last game (unless Zaire could restrict Brazil's scoring). As it happened, Yugoslavia scored first and, although Jordan equalized, this goal proved to be Scotland's undoing. Brazil beat Zaire 3-0 (they were held to 1-0 at half-time) and their goal difference (3-0) was fractionally better than Scotland's (3-1). So the Scots went wearily home although they were the only undefeated side to fail to reach the second round.

In Group One, Australia were making their debut in the finals; but they and Chile were outclassed by West and East Germany who had already qualified when they met in Hamburg on 22 June for their first international. A goal by Sparwasser in the 82nd minute gave first blood to the East. In Group Three, the Dutch started elegantly against Uruguay, who had Castillo sent off. (He was not the first to be dismissed: the Chilean Caszely had received his marching orders, against West Germany, and so had Ndaye, of Zaire.) Holland and Sweden went forward.

In Group Four, Poland were conclusive winners, scoring 12 goals against three. They were joined in the second stage by Argentina, who edged through on goal difference with Italy and Haiti out.

And so to the regroupings. In Group A Holland and Brazil won their first two games against Argentina and East Germany so their clash in Dortmund was for a place in the final. The Brazilians resorted to force (although the Dutch were no angels). Cruyff was rugby tackled by Ze Maria; Neeskens was knocked cold by Marinho behind the referee's back and

finally Luis Pereira became the fifth player to be sent off in the tournament, for a foul on Neeskens. At least the quality of the Dutch goals, by Neeskens and Cruyff, made amends.

Group B had also turned into a semi-final after West Germany and Poland had each beaten Sweden and Yugoslavia. On a rain-drenched Frankfurt pitch, Müller scored the only goal for West Germany, whose improved form in this second series was due partly to the inclusion of Bonhof in midfield. Poland's compensation was to win a dull third-place play-off against Brazil.

In the final in Munich, English referee Jack Taylor boldly awarded a penalty to Holland in the first minute after Cruyff had been brought down by Hoeness. Neeskens scored and the Dutch sat back, playing prettily without threatening another goal. After 25 minutes West Germany were level with a Breitner penalty after Holzenbein had been tripped by Jansen. On a break-away, Rep spurned an easy chance for Holland and Müller made them pay when

The master in defence: Beckenbauer (5) heads clear from the Dutch striker Rep in the 1974 finals. As 'libero' Beckenbauer was the architect of West Germany's win.

he turned on a halfpenny on a Bonhof cross to score the West German winner two minutes from half-time. The 'total football' of the Dutch – which meant that anyone could play anywhere – was defeated by the specialist skills of Müller, not forgetting the goalkeeping of Maier, the midfield strength of Bonhof, the wingplay of Grabowski and Holzenbein and, above all, the cool mastery of Beckenbauer, a survivor of 1966 and the best player in the championship alongside Cruyff.

GROUP ONE

W. Germany 1	Chile 0		E. Germany 1	Chile 1
W. Germany 2	Australia 0		E. Germany 1	W. Germany 0
W. Germany 3	Australia 0		Chile 0	Australia 0

	P	W	D	L	F	A	Pts
East Germany	3	2	1	0	4	1	5
West Germany	3	2	0	1	4	1	4
Chile	3	0	2	1	1	2	2
Australia	3	0	1	2	0	5	1

The golden goal; Dieter Müller, the German goal machine, takes a firm hold on the new World Cup trophy after West Germany's win over Holland in the 1974 final.

GROUP TWO

Brazil 0   Yugoslavia 0
Scotland 2   Zaire 0
Brazil 0   Scotland 0

Yugoslavia 9   Zaire 0
Scotland 1   Yugoslavia 1
Brazil 3   Zaire 0

	P	W	D	L	F	A	Pts
Yugoslavia	3	1	2	0	10	1	4
Brazil	3	1	2	0	3	0	4
Scotland	3	1	2	0	3	1	4
Zaire	3	0	0	3	0	14	0

GROUP THREE

Holland 2   Uruguay 0
Sweden 0   Bulgaria 0
Holland 0   Sweden 0

Bulgaria 1   Uruguay 1
Holland 4   Bulgaria 1
Sweden 3   Uruguay 0

	P	W	D	L	F	A	Pts
Holland	3	2	1	0	6	1	5
Sweden	3	1	2	0	3	0	4
Bulgaria	3	0	2	1	2	5	2
Uruguay	3	0	1	2	1	6	1

GROUP FOUR

Italy 3   Haiti 1

Poland 3   Argentina 2

Argentina 1   Italy 1
Poland 7   Haiti 0

Argentina 4   Haiti 1
Poland 2   Italy 1

	P	W	D	L	F	A	Pts
Poland	3	3	0	0	12	3	6
Argentina	3	1	1	1	7	5	3
Italy	3	1	1	1	5	4	3
Haiti	3	0	0	3	2	14	0

GROUP A

Brazil 1   E. Germany 0
Holland 4   Argentina 0
Holland 2   E. Germany 0

Brazil 2   Argentina 1
Holland 2   Brazil 0
Argentina 1   E. Germany 1

	P	W	D	L	F	A	Pts
Holland	3	3	0	0	8	0	6
Brazil	3	2	0	1	3	3	4
East Germany	3	0	1	2	1	4	1
Argentina	3	0	1	2	2	7	1

GROUP B

Poland 1   Sweden 0
W. Germany 2   Yugoslavia 0
Poland 2   Yugoslavia 1

W. Germany 4   Sweden 2
Sweden 2   Yugoslavia 1
W. Germany 1   Poland 0

	P	W	D	L	F	A	Pts
West Germany	3	3	0	0	7	2	6
Poland	3	2	0	1	3	2	4
Sweden	3	1	0	2	4	6	2
Yugoslavia	3	0	0	3	2	6	0

THIRD PLACE MATCH (Munich)
Poland 1   Brazil 0

FINAL (Munich, 7 July 1974)
W. Germany (2) 2   Holland (1) 1

West Germany: Maier; Vogts, Schwarzenbeck, Beckenbauer, Breitner, Bonhof, Hoeness, Overath, Grabowski, Müller, Holzenbein.

Holland: Jongbloed; Suurbier, Rijsbergen (De Jong), Haan, Krol, Jansen, Van Hanegem, Neeskens, Rep, Cruyff, Rensenbrink (Van der Kerkhof R).

Scorers: Breitner (*pen*), Müller for West Germany; Neeskens (*pen*) for Holland.

Leading scorer: Lato (Poland) 7.

ARGENTINA 1978

There were even more misgivings in Europe about Argentina than there had been about Mexico. There was raging inflation and widespread urban guerrilla warfare involving kidnappings and political assassinations. The go-ahead was given by FIFA in 1977 although there were rumblings in France, Holland and Sweden about a possible boycott.

There was also concern about the pressure which would be put on referees and the crude cynicism of recent Argentine teams. Argentina's gaunt, chain-smoking manager, Cesar Menotti, declared that he would have his team playing attacking football and he surprised many by recalling only three exiles from Europe; of these only Mario Kempes was available in the end. Kempes was the star of a tournament in

Above: fly the flag: Argentine fans show undying fervour for the team. Their devoted support was a key factor in Argentina's success in 1978.

Left: Ossie beats his man: Osvaldo Ardiles goes past Scirea of Italy in the first round of the 1978 finals. Italy won this match 1-0 but Argentina went on to win the title without another defeat. Ardiles should have an important part to play for Argentina in Spain.

which only a handful of teams showed true World Cup final form. The 17-year-old Argentine prodigy, Diego Maradona, was also omitted by Menotti.

Three of the best teams were in Group One – Argentina, France and Italy – and with Hungary the fourth member there would be no easy passage into the next series of league matches. (The same system as in 1974 was used.) France scored after 40 seconds against Italy but lost; Hungary had Torocsik and Nyilasi sent off in their defeat by Argentina and then lost to Italy. Against Argentina, France were again unlucky: a cruel penalty was given against them at a critical time and they were denied much better claims for a penalty at the other end. Fears about intimidated referees seemed justified. Italy beat the hosts in the last group game but both teams had already qualified.

Group Two contained two weak teams, in Tunisia and Mexico, and was a gift for West Germany and Holland. At least Tunisia covered themselves with glory by beating Mexico and holding the Germans to a draw. Group Three was closely fought with not more than one goal between the teams in any match. Brazil were uninspired but they just did enough to go through with Austria, one of the livelier teams in the series. Brazil might have lost to Spain but they were let off the hook when Cardenosa was put clean through by Santillana but fluffed the chance.

Group Four contained the sad saga of Scotland, the only British representatives (after England had been eliminated in the pre-qualifying stages by Italy, and Northern Ireland had succumbed to the Dutch). The Scots and their ebullient but inexperienced manager, Ally MacLeod,

Dutch despair: Kempes puts Argentina 2-1 ahead in extra-time against Holland in the 1978 final with his second goal of the match. Bertoni scored the third and Holland were swamped. The pitch is littered with tickertape.

arrived breathing hot air and left with their tails between their legs. They lost to Peru, 3-1, after scoring first through Jordan, but Masson missed a penalty with the score at 1-1 and Cubillas notched two goals in five minutes to sink Scotland. After the game a dope test on Willie Johnston proved positive and he was banned from internationals for a year. Scotland sent him home saying that he could never play for them again. The Scots slumped to a draw in their next match against humble Iran (even the Scottish goal was an own goal). However, when all was almost lost they bounced back to beat Holland 3-2 in their last match. Souness was picked in midfield at long last and Gemmill crowned a fine performance with a brilliant individual goal. Earlier, Holland had taken the lead through a Rensenbrink penalty, Dalglish had equalized and Gemmill had put Scotland ahead with another penalty when Souness was fouled. Finally Rep scored from long range and the Dutch qualified on goal difference.

In the second series, Holland played much better to reach the final, hitting five goals against Austria, holding West Germany in a 2-2 draw and beating Italy (a draw would have been enough for the Dutch although they had won only two of their six games – a clear indictment of the system). In Group B, Brazil and Argentina were left with a goal-scoring competition after they had contested a sour, scoreless draw. Brazil beat Poland in the afternoon, 3-1, leaving Argentina to score at least four times that evening against Peru whose eccentric goalkeeper, Quiroga, was Argentine-born. (Nicknamed 'El Loco', Quiroga had been booked against Poland for a rugby tackle in his *opponents'* half.) Argentina were irresistible, winning 6-0.

The start of the final in Buenos Aires was delayed for 10 minutes while Argentina complained about the plaster cast on Rene Van der Kerkhof's wrist. Kempes won the match which went to extra-time: his first-half goal was cancelled seven minutes from time by Nanninga for Holland, but in the extra period Kempes scored again and set up a simple third goal for Bertoni. So the host nation had won for the third time in four World Cups.

GROUP ONE

Italy 2	France 1	Argentina 2	France 1
Argentina 2	Hungary 1	France 3	Hungary 1
Italy 3	Hungary 1	Italy 1	Argentina 0

	P	W	D	L	F	A	Pts
Italy	3	3	0	0	6	2	6
Argentina	3	2	0	1	4	3	4
France	3	1	0	2	5	5	2
Hungary	3	0	0	3	3	8	0

GROUP TWO

W. Germany 0 Poland 0
Tunisia 3 Mexico 1
Poland 1 Tunisia 0
W. Germany 6 Mexico 0
Poland 3 Mexico 1
W. Germany 0 Tunisia 0

	P	W	D	L	F	A	Pts
Poland	3	2	1	0	4	1	5
West Germany	3	1	2	0	6	0	4
Tunisia	3	1	1	1	3	2	3
Mexico	3	0	0	3	2	12	0

GROUP THREE

Austria 2 Spain 1
Brazil 1 Sweden 1
Austria 1 Sweden 0
Brazil 0 Spain 0
Spain 1 Sweden 0
Brazil 1 Austria 0

	P	W	D	L	F	A	Pts
Austria	3	2	0	1	3	2	4
Brazil	3	1	2	0	2	1	4
Spain	3	1	1	1	2	2	3
Sweden	3	0	1	2	1	3	1

GROUP FOUR

Peru 3 Scotland 1
Holland 3 Iran 0
Scotland 1 Iran 1
Holland 0 Peru 0
Peru 4 Iran 1
Scotland 3 Holland 2

	P	W	D	L	F	A	Pts
Peru	3	2	1	0	7	2	5
Holland	3	1	1	1	5	3	3
Scotland	3	1	1	1	5	6	3
Iran	3	0	1	2	2	8	1

GROUP A

W. Germany 0 Italy 0
Holland 5 Austria 1
Italy 1 Austria 0
Holland 2 W. Germany 2
Holland 2 Italy 1
Austria 3 W. Germany 2

	P	W	D	L	F	A	Pts
Holland	3	2	1	0	9	4	5
Italy	3	1	1	1	2	2	3
West Germany	3	0	2	1	4	5	2
Austria	3	1	0	2	4	8	2

GROUP B

Brazil 3 Peru 0
Argentina 2 Poland 0
Poland 1 Peru 0
Argentina 0 Brazil 0
Brazil 3 Poland 1
Argentina 6 Peru 0

	P	W	D	L	F	A	Pts
Argentina	3	2	1	0	8	0	5
Brazil	3	2	1	0	6	1	5
Poland	3	1	0	2	2	5	2
Peru	3	0	0	3	0	10	0

THIRD PLACE MATCH (Buenos Aires)
Brazil 2 Italy 1

FINAL (Buenos Aires, 25 June 1978)
Argentina (1) (1) 3 Holland (0) (1) 1 aet

Argentina: Fillol; Olguin, Galvan L., Passarella, Tarantini, Ardiles (Larrosa), Gallego, Ortiz (Houseman), Bertoni, Luque, Kempes.

Holland: Jongbloed; Krol, Poortvliet, Brandts, Jansen (Suurbier), Haan, Neeskens, Van der Kerkhof W., Rep (Nanninga), Van der Kerkhof R., Rensenbrink.

Scorers: Kempes 2, Bertoni for Argentina; Nanninga for Holland.

Leading scorer: Kempes (Argentina) 6.

GOALSCORING AND ATTENDANCES IN WORLD CUP FINAL ROUNDS

		Matches	Goals (average)	Attendance (average)
1930	Uruguay	18	70 (3.8)	434,500 (24,138)
1934	Italy	17	70 (4.1)	395,000 (23,235)
1938	France	18	84 (4.6)	483,000 (26,833)
1950	Brazil	22	88 (4.0)	1,337,000 (60,772)
1954	Switzerland	26	140 (5.3)	943,000 (36,270)
1958	Sweden	35	126 (3.6)	868,000 (24,800)
1962	Chile	32	89 (2.7)	776,000 (24,250)
1966	England	32	89 (2.7)	1,614,677 (50,458)
1970	Mexico	32	95 (2.9)	1,673,975 (52,311)
1974	West Germany	38	97 (2.5)	1,774,022 (46,684)
1978	Argentina	38	102 (2.6)	1,610,215 (42,374)

Spain are worthy hosts for the 12th World Cup. They have the background of a great footballing nation and they have the facilities to stage the biggest soccer tournament of all time.

Spain's glowing reputation in world soccer is founded on the exploits of their great clubs. Pride of place must go to Real Madrid, European champions from 1956 to 1960 with one of the most brilliant teams ever assembled by a soccer club. Real were

Where they play

Group One will be played at La Caruña and Vigo in the northwest. Italy is the seeded nation. The stadiums are the Riazor in La Coruña and Balaidos in Vigo and the June climate is relatively cool with temperatures averaging 17°C (the mid-60s F).

Group Two is in Oviedo and Gijon in the north. West Germany are the seeds. The stadiums are the Carlos Tartiere in Oviedo and El Molinon in Gijon and the players will face a similar climate to Group One.

Group Three includes holders Argentina. These matches are in the warmer Mediterranean climes of Alicante (which boasts 272 days of sunshine in a year) at the Jose Rico Perez stadium, opened in 1974. Also at Elche where the new 50,000 capacity new Stadium was opened in 1976.

Group Four is reserved for England in Bilbao, capital of the Basque country, and Valladolid. There has been concern that Basque separatists would use the World Cup for political propaganda. This was intensified by the kidnapping of the Barcelona forward Enrique Castro ('Quini') for 25 days in 1981. But Joao Havelange, the president of FIFA, said that there was no cause for alarm as 'sport is nothing to do with politics'. The Basques have since stated that they will not disrupt the World Cup, although doubts linger. England will be based in Athletic Bilbao's San Mames Stadium. A new stadium costing £½m has been built in Valladolid. Mean temperatures at about 18°C.

Group Five (Spain are the seeds) is in Valencia's Luis Casanova Stadium and the enlarged La Romareda Stadium in Zaragoza.

Group Six (Brazil) is at the Benito Villamarin Stadium, Seville, the home of the Real Betis club (two matches), at the Sanchez Pizjuan Stadium (one match), the home of Seville FC and at La Rosaleda Stadium, Malaga.

also European champions in 1966 and runners-up in 1962 and 1964: they were also runners-up in the European Cup Winners' Cup in 1971 and they have been Spanish champions 20 times since that league first began in 1929.

The dazzling Real Madrid of the 1950s was a cosmopolitan collection of talent. In their famous all-white strip they overwhelmed their opponents with attacking football. Apart from their home-grown stars Gento and Del Sol, Real had household names such as di Stefano and Rial from Argentina, Puskas from Hungary, Kopa from France, and José Santamaria from Uruguay (now Spain's manager). This glittering array achieved the heights in 1960. They astounded a crowd of 127,621 at Hampden Park, in the European Cup Final when they defeated Eintracht Frankfurt 7-3 in a soccer classic. They later became the first World Club champions.

The first team to beat Real in Europe were their great Spanish rivals Barcelona. They were founded in 1899, three years before Real Madrid, by Hans Gamper, a Swiss, and they were the runners-up in the first Spanish Cup final in 1902. They also spread their net wide to pull together a successful team in the 1950s. The Barcelona side which ended Real Madrid's winning sequence in the European Cup included the Hungarians, Kocsis and Czibor, from the great 1954 World Cup team. They have never reached the heights of Real Madrid but in 1979 they won the European Cupwinners' Cup with a typically multinational team, including the Dutchman Neeskens and the Austrian Krankl. They also won the European Fairs Cup (now the Uefa Cup) three times.

Real Madrid and Barcelona are not the only noteworthy Spanish clubs. Athletic Bilbao are Spain's oldest club, founded in 1898. They have won the league six times but are more renowned as cup cam-

The 14 venues around Spain

ALICANTE	JOSE RICO PEREZ	**MALAGA**	LA ROSALEDA
BARCELONA	R.C.D. ESPAÑOL	**OVIEDO**	CARLOS TARTIERE
	NOU CAMP	**SEVILLA**	SANCHEZ PIZJUAN
BILBAO	SAN MAMES		BENITO VILLAMARIN
ELCHE	NUEVO ESTADIO	**VALENCIA**	LUIS CASANOVA
GIJON	EL MOLINON	**VALLADOLID**	EL PRADO
LA CORUNA	RIAZOR	**VIGO**	BALAIDOS
MADRID	SANTIAGO BERNABEU	**ZARAGOZA**	LA ROMAREDA
	VINCENTE CALDERON		

39

paigners. They have lifted the Spanish cup 24 times and in 1977 were losing finalists to Juventus in the Uefa Cup. Bilbao, where England will play their first phase matches, have had an English approach to soccer from their early years, when they were guided by Arthur Pentland, to the present day. For a time they had as manager Ronnie Allen who is now in charge of the English first division club West Bromwich Albion.

Spanish success in the Fairs Cup in the 1960s was maintained by Valencia, who won the trophy in 1963 and 1964 and lost the 1965 final to compatriots Real Zaragoza. Recently Valencia have had the services of Kempes, the star of Argentina's World Cup winning side in 1978, and the West German Bonhof. They helped beat Arsenal on penalties in the final of the 1980 Cupwinners' Cup. Atlético Madrid have

occasionally emerged from the shadow of their illustrious neighbours to gain honours such as the European Cupwinners' Cup in 1962 and to reach the European Cup final in 1974.

The record of Spanish club teams has not been matched by their national side. The first Spanish side to play international soccer was in the 1920 Olympics. They won the silver medal in a competition re-arranged after the withdrawal of Czechoslovakia. Spain were the first country to defeat England in an international 4-3 in Madrid in 1929. In 1934 they forced fancied Italy to a replay in their first World Cup finals. In 1950 they finished fourth, eliminating England in the first phase. They also qualified for the finals in 1962, 1966 and 1978 without setting the world alight.

One of Spain's best performances was winning the European Nations Cup in

Below: the final stage: the San Bernabeu Stadium, home of Real Madrid, photographed from the air. This is the setting for some second-phase matches and for the final itself which takes place at 8 pm on Sunday 11 July 1982.

Right: the opening scene: the Nou Camp Stadium, home of Barcelona FC, where the opening ceremony and some second-phase matches are being held; the winners of Groups A and C meet here in their semi-final.

1964. They defeated Russia 2-1 in the final in Madrid and their team included two of the country's great players – Amancio and Suarez who was transferred from Barcelona to Inter Milan in 1961 for a then world record fee of £200,000.

The natural flair and individuality of Spanish-based footballers is reflected by the success of their players in the European Footballer of the Year poll. From 1957 to 1960 the award was won in turn by di Stefano, Kopa, di Stefano and Suarez (who was twice second and once third in the rankings).

It was with this background that Spain put themselves forward in 1964 as candidates to host the World Cup. West Germany were also in the running that year and FIFA selected them to stage the World Cup for 1974. But when the international federation met during the 1966 finals in England there was no opposition to Spain being hosts in 1982.

A more controversial decision at a later FIFA congress was to allow 24 nations to compete in Spain. This was an attempt to ensure a more balanced finals. As the qualifying competiton is arranged on a zonal basis, it is inevitable that some relatively weak soccer nations reach the finals while stronger ones are left on the sidelines. Thus England failed to qualify in 1974 but Haiti and Australia were in the finals; in 1978 again England and Uruguay were absent while Iran and Tunisia took part. In 1982 Holland – runners up in 1974 and 1978 – failed to qualify but Cameroon, Algeria, Honduras, Kuwait and New Zealand will be the minnows in the big soccer bowl.

The world soccer powers had no wish to decry the merits of Haiti, Australia, Iran or Tunisia. Indeed, it is essential that new blood should be injected if soccer is to justify its claim to be the world game. But there was also a strong argument that the finals should be contested by as many of the best teams as possible. There is no easy answer. The decision to have 24 teams in Spain will mean that the 1982 finals will be spread over 29 days and include 52 matches. Fortunately, Spain are well endowed with fine stadiums.

SPAIN

Colours: red shirts, dark blue shorts (*reserve colours:* blue shirts, dark blue shorts)

Of the eleven World Cup competitions played since 1930, the hosts have won five including the last two in Argentina and West Germany. So Spain enjoy a big advantage but suffer the pressure of being expected to do well. The question is whether their football can justify their automatic position among the favourites.

Like the holders, Argentina, Spain have gone straight to the finals without having to qualify. In escaping the preliminaries, they have missed the valuable benefits of stiff competition. Their preparations have been in friendly matches which are rarely as keen. The main challengers will be West Germany, Brazil and Argentina.

With warm weather and excitable crowds, the conditions in Spain will not be as strange to the South Americans as they were in previous more northerly finals. Yet the Spanish team can claim to have the best of both worlds because the man in charge of their challenge is the famous former Real Madrid player, José Santamaria, who is of Uruguayan origin. He has found the job full of problems.

Spain made little impression on the 1978 competition in Argentina where they found their best form too late. They failed to win a match in the European Championship in Italy but they won compliments for some sparkling football. For all the inventive play of Zamora, in midfield, and Satrustegui, in attack, especially against the Italians, the team failed to score enough goals. This has been a worrying restriction to Santamaria's progress. At times potential goalscorers have been afraid to risk taking half-chances.

Santamaria's position was precarious when potentially his best team only drew 0-0 with Austria early in this season. A 3-0 win over Luxembourg did not convince the critics, although some were happy to see the young but experienced striker Lopez Ufarte return and score two goals. The manager was in the middle of internal arguments. Fans everywhere want to see their favourites included in their team. But this is intensified in Spain by strong regional feelings. So when he dropped the skilful Real Madrid player, Juanito, the critics became even more cutting.

A 3-2 win over Poland in Lodz was badly needed to help raise confidence but Spain still have to be inspired by the occasion. Four years ago, Argentina gave them a perfect example of how to win the championship by extracting the best from their players at exactly the right moment. Spain have players of similar temperament to the volatile Argentines and if several strike top form at the same time they will be formidable opponents.

Many of the squad members are highly talented ball players. Juanito was not at his best at the beginning of the season but this clever and temperamental winger has the ability to turn the direction of a match in a single move. He can form a dangerous partnership with the Real Madrid centre forward, Santillana, who is particularly strong when the ball is in the air.

Juanito and Zamora were the architects of a fine 2-1 win over England at Wembley in March 1981. The victory by a new, young side was a great boost, but England played poorly, giving too much freedom to Juanito

On the ball: Zamora, the inventive midfield player for Real Sociedad and Spain, who should provide plenty of sparkle for the host nation and will leave visiting defences flat.

in particular.

Spain have said they will play attacking football in the style of the sixties (when they won the European Championship) but they know that to reach the final they must tighten their defence. Their gifted and experienced goalkeeper, Arconada, has all too often been left without adequate cover. In Gordillo, they have one of the quickest defenders in Europe and Alesanco has always enjoyed speeding upfield to score a goal or two. That can leave the comparatively young Tendillo with too much responsibility. Defenders who so enjoy counter-attacking can be a mixed blessing. In Group Five in the finals Yugoslavia and Northern Ireland will hope to exploit any chinks in the Spanish defence.

In their best performances Spain have been well served in midfield by Zamora and Alonso, club colleagues at Real Sociedad. Zamora was the winning goalscorer in the victory over England last year. Even so Santamaria admitted much work had to be done. A tour to South America did little to encourage him, except in Brazil where the defenders tackled hard and kept control over Zico and Socrates.

'Olé': Juanito shows who is boss. He will be an important figure for Spain if they are to succeed this summer in front of their expectant fans. He and Zamora were architects of Spain's 2-1 victory over England at Wembley.

ARGENTINA

Colours: blue and white striped shirts, black shorts (*reserve colours:* all blue)

Only one South American team, Pelé's Brazil in 1958, have ever won the World Cup in Europe. Only Italy and Brazil have successfully defended the trophy. So for Argentina the task in Spain is immense.

Since beating Holland 3-1 after extra-time in Buenos Aires four years ago, the world champions have built on their success by winning the World Youth Cup. There is no doubt that young, clever players continue to be produced in Argentina. But manager Cesar Menotti has had the job of keeping the best of the winning 1978 team playing together. These days footballers know the value of fame and are not content to stay at home if they can earn much bigger salaries abroad.

Soon after the last World Cup Menotti's exciting team broke up. Little Ardiles, an artist in midfield, went to England only two weeks after the final. Villa, a useful member of the squad, joined him. Kempes, the leading goalscorer, rejoined Valencia before later returning to Argentina. But there was consolation. The exceptionally gifted Diego Maradona, who won his first cap at only 16, was kept back from the finals in his own country because he lacked experience. His game has developed enormously and now he is regarded as the top player in the world. Is he the new Pelé? Absolute proof should come on the World Cup stage.

Maradona and Menotti fell out last year.

Yesterday's hero: Kempes is striving to find fitness for 1982 after being the undoubted star and leading goalscorer for Argentina in the 1978 finals. After a spell with Valencia he has returned home in his quest for peak form. It is important for Argentina that he should do so.

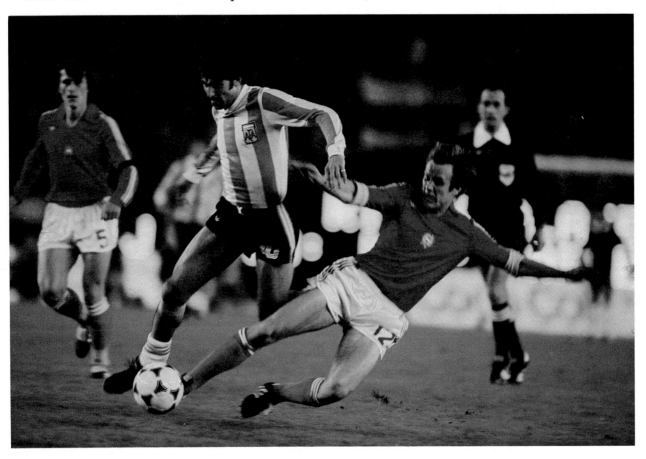

45

Maradona failed to turn up for training and for a brief period was out of the squad. Menotti said it was the player's choice. Certainly Argentina's noisy supporters soon yelled for his return when the team lost at home to Poland 2-1 (their first defeat in three years). This was followed by a 1-1 draw with Czechoslovakia.

Menotti's most important opportunity to re-establish the World Cup winning team was in the Gold Cup event held in Montevideo early in 1981. Argentina beat Switzerland 5-0 and drew with the improving Russians immediately before the tournament. But they were criticized for being only as good as Maradona played, or was allowed to play by ruthless defenders. Menotti has tried to encourage youth in the shape of Diaz, centre forward in the successful youth team. He has also backed experience by retaining Passarella as captain in the defence.

For Argentina the Gold Cup tournament was tainted by the sight of Maradona and Tarantini involved in a massive fight after a 1-1 draw with Brazil (who went on to lose to Uruguay in the final). But the Argentines displayed such eloquent football in their match against West Germany that they must be candidates to win another World Cup. To many observers Maradona's snatches of magical skill proved he was the best player in the world. Unhappily, Kempes, the dynamic force in 1978, limped off the field. But even without him, Argentina recovered from Germany's first-half headed goal by Hrubesch to score twice in the final six minutes.

In the Gold Cup matches, organized for winners of the World Cup, Menotti was not pleased with the performances of the players who had left Argentina to seek their fortunes in Europe. Even Ardiles, who had become such a favourite in the English league with Tottenham Hotspur,

Top dogs: Argentina's Gold Cup team of 1981 (standing, left to right): Passarella, Bertoni, Olguin, Galvin, Tarantini, Fillol and (in front) Gallego, Barbas, Diaz, Maradona and Ardiles. The defending champions hope to become the first South American nation since Brazil to win in Europe.

Diego Maradona

Football's relentless need for stars brings a heavy toll. Young players crack under the pressure. Maradona is the brightest star in the soccer solar system and the most vulnerable. Towards the end of Argentina's World Cup build-up he found the strain too great and asked to be dropped.

Descended from Italian immigrants, Maradona comes from a large family in Buenos Aires. His father was a railway worker who played football at a modest level. Diego joined the Argentinos Juniors club early in his teens and was encouraged by Vittorio Spinetto's coaching.

He hardly looked the part of a future world-beater. He was short, and is still only 5 ft 4 in, but became muscular, tough and amazingly quick with the ball. His first appearance for Argentinos Juniors' top team came at the age of only 16, in 1977. His fame spread so rapidly that he was soon the most popular player in the country. Offers came from abroad. Barcelona wanted him for £1 million. Argentinos Juniors paid him £150,000 a year and said he was not for sale.

Maradona won his first cap at 16. His reputation grew with electrifying flashes of attacking midfield play in the Gold Cup tournament in 1981 and on tour in Europe. At home he endured all the problems of being the number one attraction. Finally he told the Argentine FA that if he were to stay in the country they had to make an alternative offer to Barcelona's latest bid. Argentinos Juniors were loaned money to provide him with the 'compensation'.

There were more complications when his club and Boca Juniors were involved in a loan transaction. The deal was said to be worth £4 millions and involved other players. The pressure became too much. Maradona asked to be left out of the Argentine training sessions. Without him the team played poorly against Czechoslovakia and Poland and the public demanded his return. There is little doubt he will play in Spain but the question is whether there, too, the demands will be too much.

Cesar Luis Menotti

The tall, lean chain-smoking architect of Argentina's victory in 1978, Menotti has been brave when necessary, not least when holding back Maradona from the 1978 finals. He has also made important U-turns. Originally he intended to restrict the World Cup team of 1978 to home-based players. But he changed his mind and brought Mario Kempes home. In his best form, Kempes will be a priceless asset to Menotti in Spain.

Menotti comes from Rosario. His arrival in full-time football was at the comparatively late age of 22, after he had trained as a chemical engineer. He played with Union Americana of Rosario as a teenager but later joined Velez Sarsfield. He returned to Rosario to play for Central as a half-back. His playing career also took him to Racing in Buenos Aires, Boca Juniors, New York and eventually Santos in Brazil. He finished with Juventus of Sao Paolo.

As a coach Menotti started with Newells Old Boys before joining Huracan who became Argentine champions in 1973. He was offered the position as Argentina's coach in 1974.

Until he plotted Argentina's path to World Cup glory he was constantly criticized. He overcame domestic difficulties, including a reluctance by the authorities to alter club fixtures to suit international plans. He repaid the Argentine FA for their eventual cooperation by assembling a team good enough to win the World Cup. The 1978 team kept up a frantic pace but in Spain the latest side will probably return to their traditional stop-go rhythm. The 1982 side is certain to bear striking similarity to the 1978 side.

Previous pages: shooting star: even when surrounded by Irishmen Daly, Moran and Langan, Maradona manages to get in a shot at goal.

Above: no entry: Hungary's Nyilasi stretches to cut off Argentina's Ardiles in full flight in the 1978 World Cup. Nyilasi and Torocsik were sent off in this match.

was told he was playing too many 'safe' passes and that he should spend his time hitting the ball forward and moving for the return in order to unsettle defenders. This was the value of Ardiles in 1978 and there is now the exciting prospect of an Ardiles-Maradona partnership in Spain.

Menotti is hoping that in Spain his team will rediscover their winning formula and again leave opponents gasping for breath. Yet they cannot expect referees in Spain to be as lenient as in 1978. The length of the tournament may also mean team changes along the way.

WEST GERMANY

Colours: white shirts, black shorts (*reserve colours:* green shirts, white shorts)

Even before the qualifying competition began West Germany were among the clear favourites to win the World Cup. Certainly they are the best of the European contenders and they have been given a favourable draw. At the time of the draw they had more clubs involved in European club cup competitions than any other country. They won the European Championship in 1980 so the World Cup qualifying group offered no special problems. Even so, some Germans complained about a lack of talent.

The eight qualifying games increased the stature of the Germans. They won all of them, finishing in style with an 8-0 victory

First step to glory: West Germany go for possession in the opening game of the 1980 European Championship against Czechoslovakia.

over Albania and a 4-0 defeat of Bulgaria. They scored a total of 33 goals and conceded only three. As if to frighten the rest of Europe, and warn the world, they took off their European Footballer of the Year, Karl-Heinz Rummenigge after 50 minutes of the match against Albania. By then he had already scored a hat-trick.

Jupp Derwall, who took over as manager from Helmut Schoen in 1978, inherited a remarkable record. The Germans had never lost a qualifying tie. He maintained the record and in his first three years kept West Germany unbeaten by European sides. They finally lost their record of 23 unbeaten matches against teams from all parts of the world when visiting South America for the Gold Cup tournament.

The games between West Germany and Austria were the only World Cup qualifying matches with any threat of a surprise. West Germany cruised through the first match and won the second 3-1, despite being without Hansi Müller and Horst Hrubesch. A new talent emerged in Pierre Littbarski, a small winger who announced his international arrival by scoring two goals against Austria in Vienna. The Germans' rivalry with Austria will be renewed in Group Two in Spain.

In the European Championship final against Belgium it was Hrubesch, rather than the much praised Rummenigge, who grabbed the headlines by scoring both goals in the 2-1 victory. Even so, midfield man Bernd Schuster was the star and was brilliant in the final. His powerful shooting and rapid acceleration highlighted an otherwise ordinary tournament.

As with several other countries, the Germans hope that their most experienced players – Fischer, Hrubesch and Breitner – will be available for one last effort in Spain. Fischer is an exceptionally effective finisher, while Paul Breitner has returned to organize midfield. The overall strength runs deep.

Some critics have argued that the Gold Cup tournament merely proved that the South Americans were far ahead of the best of the Europeans in terms of skill and readiness for Spain. But it could also be argued that the competition was not taken too seriously by the Europeans for whom it was seen as useful experience but no more.

Against Argentina, West Germany played attractively, with Rummenigge often out-pacing the defence, and Briegel, a powerful former decathlete, marking Maradona more efficiently than others had done. But the heat got the better of the West

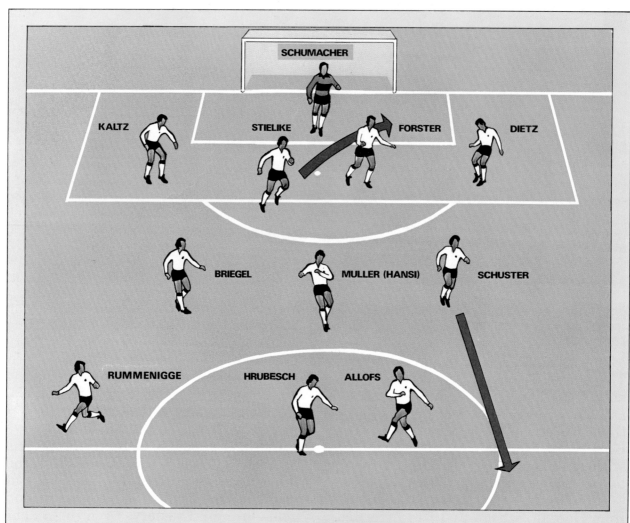

West Germany's Winning Way

This is the successful line-up for West Germany on 22 June 1980 when they beat Belgium 2-1 in the final of the European Championship. In this 4-3-3 system Stielike was the sweeper and Förster the stopper. In this match Briegel was given a special marking job on Belgium's Van Moer. Now he is more usually seen at left back and has played as sweeper as well as in midfield. He can also play on the left or right side. The 1982 line-up is likely to have Breitner back as the midfield hub. Jupp Derwall, the West German manager, has also experimented with two central strikers – Fischer and Hrubesch. Rummenigge, a natural right winger, is also a fine goalscorer. In Littbarski they have another promising winger. The German squad are so strong that they can keep their tactics fluid from one game to another. This strength enables them to keep opponents guessing about their line-up and tactical plan and they can easily adapt to 4-4-2 if necessary. They can even change in the middle of a game: in the 1980 final Briegel was injured early in the second half but West Germany survived.

Jupp Derwall

When Derwall succeeded the widely respected Helmut Schoen as manager of West Germany he was hardly known outside the country. With typical thoroughness, the Germans had planned his appointment over many years, just as they had groomed Schoen to succeed Sepp Herberger. Schoen had taken the Germans to victory in the 1972 European Championships and the 1974 World Cup. Derwall was his assistant and coach to the B team. He had been employed by the German federation for eight years. His 'apprenticeship' made the job less onerous.

As a full back he appeared in the colours of Rhenania Würselen, Alemannia Aachen, Fortuna Düsseldorf and later moved to Saarbrücken as manager. Like Schoen before him, he was appointed coach to the Saar federation, a stepping stone to the job as Schoen's assistant. In 1978 he became manager of the team who are now European favourites to win the 1982 World Cup.

Derwall is 56, grey-haired and obviously the distinguished elder statesman of the German federation. His progress in the World Cup qualifying competition suggested that all the long-term planning was bearing fruit. At least he knows that if Germany fail his job should be secure. Herberger lasted 28 years. Schoen was manager for 14 years.

Karl-Heinz Rummenigge

Rummenigge was European Footballer of the Year in 1980 and 1981. He is 26 years old, a compact, sturdy winger who sets up many of West Germany's attacks. He has also become a deadly finisher. If the Germans had allowed him to run at defences in Argentina they would have been more successful.

His fine balance and astonishing ball control were first appreciated by his home-town club, Borussia Lippstadt. At 19 he was taken on by Bayern Munich. After creating a splendid first impression with his dribbling he lost confidence and was dropped.

In 1975 he was playing in Bayern's reserves when the club beat Leeds United to win the European Cup. He worked hard at his goalscoring and reclaimed his first-team place in time to play in the final the following year when Bayern beat St Etienne to keep the trophy for a third season. It was also in 1976 that he made his debut for West Germany against Wales.

The Germans now rely on his skill as a scorer as much as a winger. In the World Cup qualifying games he was often the most effective finisher. He scored three against Finland and Albania and two against Bulgaria.

German general: Hansi Müller, who usually operates on the left side of West Germany's midfield, moves forward in the friendly against Brazil in 1981. Brazil won 1-0.

Germans and they lost 2-1, ending their long, unbeaten run. Then they went down 4-1 to Brazil.

The Brazilians also beat West Germany in Stuttgart last year when goalkeeper Schumacher and Schuster were substituted at half-time. Schuster was shortly to play for Barcelona in a Spanish Cup match and made it all too obvious. After a dis-agreement with Derwall he dropped himself from the squad, but even when he patched up the argument a knee ligament injury may have cost him his place.

This second defeat by Brazil was of greater concern to Derwall who said: 'We may lose some day against European opposition, but basically we must orientate ourselves to the South Americans if we want to be world champions'. The irony was that before the last World Cup Brazil felt they had to become more 'European'.

AUSTRIA

Colours: white shirts, black shorts (*reserve colours:* red shirts, white shorts)

In Argentina, Austria caused one of the major surprises by beating West Germany 3-2. The Germans lost their title as world champions. They had not lost to Austria since 1931 and the recriminations were bitter.

The Germans gained some revenge by winning 2-0 and 3-1 in the qualifying group for Spain. Nevertheless, Austria finished two points ahead of Albania and Finland, but dangerously close to Bulgaria.

Bruno Pezzey, who was chosen in Enzo Bearzot's World XI against Argentina on the World Cup anniversary in 1979, continues to be the outstanding member of the Austrian team. His experience in the German league has been important to the national side. There were high hopes that the goal-scoring Gernot Jurtin would become just as good, but he has had a cartilage operation. He was the leading scorer in the Austrian league in 1980-81 and had only just begun to make an impression at international level.

Austria would like to include a large number of home-based players in their team and in Christian Keglevits and Max Hagmayr they have talented prospects. An old Austrian problem is that most of the better players leave the country for better pay and greater glory. So the national team have to call up players from all parts of Europe. The difficulty in building team understanding is obvious.

Manager Karl Stotz often prepared for matches without his foreign-based players who arrived at the last moment. He still chose them but made so many other changes that 30 different players appeared in the World Cup qualifying games, bringing heavy criticism from leaders of the Austrian Football Association.

In the end Austria finished two points ahead of Bulgaria in third place. They had to wait until the very last match to be absolutely sure of a place among the final 24. Their hopes rested on their old rivals, West Germany. Bulgaria would qualify only if they could beat the Germans 6-0 in their last game. There was never any serious danger of that and the West Germans obliged the Austrians with a 4-0 victory.

Behind the scenes in Austria there was extreme anger. Although the final Group One table showed Austria comfortably placed they had to depend on West Ger-

Knees up, Bruno: the talented Austrian 'libero', Bruno Pezzey, springs into action. He is expected to be the mainspring of the Austrian machine in Spain, as he has been for several years.

many for the right result. The problem came to a head. Disagreements between Stotz and the Austrian FA continued after the qualifying games and ended with the manager being sacked after a poor goalless draw in a friendly with Spain. Ernst Happel, the former Dutch international team manager, was asked to take charge but his club, Hamburg, refused to release him.

Above; four musketeers: the Austrians Jara, Krankl, Keglevits and Welzl celebrate. Krankl (no. 9) will continue to be important to his country as a goal-getter this summer.

While Hans Krankl is now one of Europe's most experienced forwards and Prohaska and Jara can be dominating influences in midfield, Austria are unlikely to cope with the most powerful, well-tested teams in Spain.

BELGIUM

Colours: all white (*reserve colours:* red shirts, black shorts)

Belgium upstaged Holland in the European Championships by reaching the final, and now they go to Spain while their illustrious Dutch neighbours watch on television. Holland were World Cup runners-up in 1974 and 1978 when Belgium did not even qualify.

In the European Championship they drew 1-1 with England, beat Spain 2-1 and held Italy to a goalless draw to reach a final with West Germany. Although they lost 2-1, their strong second-half recovery proved their worth. Their performances

Opposite: happy Belgium: (left to right) Gerets, Vandenbergh, and Van Moer celebrate during their country's friendly against Poland in 1980. Little Van Moer is 36 but will be in the squad, if only to give advice.

56

throughout were practical. The experience of Julien Cools was invaluable, especially in the game against Spain when he scored the winning goal. A year earlier his club, Brugge, had released him on a free transfer.

Belgium qualified for Spain from Group Two even before they went to play in Holland last October. They were the first European team to do so although placed in a difficult qualifying group, with Holland, the excellent Republic of Ireland side, and France.

France beat Belgium 3-2 in Paris. The Belgians knew that they had to beat France in the return match in Brussels in September to avoid visiting Holland in need of two points. Gerets and Vandereycken were both injured so Renquin was moved to right back and Alex Czerniatynski, the son of a Polish migrant, was given his first match on the right wing. Despite the changes, the Belgians were well organized but the French showed a marked lack of understanding.

Czerniatynski had a memorable day,

scoring a simple first goal and making the second for Vandenbergh who made sure that Belgium qualified. Little Wilfried Van Moer, aged 36, said it was his last international match, but manager Guy Thys asked him to be a member of the World Cup squad if only to give advice.

In an early 1-1 draw with the Republic of Ireland in Dublin, Thys showed that he could get by without Cools and Van der Elst, who were not available. The re-arranged team also suggested that the players had lost none of the aggression seen during the European Championship. Their uncompromising approach was again seen in a home 1-0 victory over the Dutch.

Belgium will not be an easy side to beat in Spain, but the competition will demand more energy than the European Championship. The standard of play will be higher and the older players may find it all too much. Argentina and Hungary will provide an early test of their mettle in Spain.

Belgian break: Ceulemans goes past the fallen figure of Förster in the 1980 European final against West Germany. Stielike is no. 15.

FRANCE

Colours: blue shirts, white shorts (*reserve colours:* red shirts, white shorts)

Before the 1978 World Cup finals, France were generally regarded as one of the most attractive and promising of the European challengers. They had the excellent Michel Platini in midfield, the sturdy Marius Tresor in defence and the speed of Dominique Rocheteau in attack. In their first game, against Italy, they scored inside 40 seconds.

They were in Argentina's group and they went out when beaten 2-1 by the hosts in a highly controversial game which included a doubtful penalty. Everyone, except Argentina, agreed that the tournament was the poorer for losing this attractive side.

This time they should not be so intimi-

The 29-year-old Alain Giresse, the attacking French midfield player, takes on Cyprus during the World Cup qualifying match in December 1981.

dated and, with any luck, will not suffer so much questionable refereeing. The question now is whether they still have such a good team. Few good sides remain at their peak for four years.

At face value they will be a substantial threat. They proved their worth by qualifying out of a strong group that included the Dutch World Cup runners-up, the Belgian European Championship runners-up and the Republic of Ireland, a fine side, even if some of the players had the most tenuous of Irish connections.

France finally eliminated the declining Dutch in Paris in November 1981. Tresor, Rocheteau and Bernard Lacombe were recalled. Platini and Didier Six, also survivors of the team of four years ago, were the scorers in a 2-0 win. Platini curled in one of his famous free-kicks and Rocheteau created the second. France were left needing to beat Cyprus in Paris to pass the Irish

on goal difference. Cyprus had not won a match and, predictably, lost 4-0.

Michel Hidalgo, the French team manager, has not had a straightforward task. Tresor, so powerful and dominating in Argentina, has not been fully fit. Bathenay, the strength of the side in midfield, has been below his best. Rocheteau missed the important game in Dublin where Hidalgo was criticized for trying new players. One of the newcomers, Bruno Bellone, scored an astonishing goal in a 3-2

Michel Platini

Midfield inspiration of St Etienne and France, Platini appears to control time. He combines subtlety, vision and stamina. He is also the finest exponent, outside South America, of the direct free-kick.

His shrewd passing from midfield was particularly evident in France's later qualifying matches, but his 'dead ball' kick will be most feared by defences in Spain. Although a provider and creator, he has also been the highest scorer in the French league.

Aged 27, Platini was born in Joeuf and originally played for Nancy. He made his first appearance for France against Czechoslovakia in 1976; since then he has been the subject of numerous offers from foreign clubs. He joined St Etienne in 1979, although he had received offers from Inter-Milan. At times he must have been tempted to leave, especially when St Etienne began to decline. Some of the fans seemed to blame him personally for every mistake made by the team as a whole.

At times he has been asked to act as France's centre forward but he is at his most dangerous moving forward from deeper positions. In Spain, he should be recognized as one of Europe's outstanding modern schemers.

defeat. Receiving the ball from Couriol, he left Langan flat-footed and beat goalkeeper McDonagh from the edge of the penalty area.

Hidalgo had earlier put Platini at centre forward against the Belgians in Brussels, bringing more criticism. France lost 2-0, assuring Belgium of a place in the finals. Confident goalkeeping by Pierrick Hiard, another of their new players, saved France from an even more damaging defeat.

While some of the established players have lost their edge, one or two of the younger ones show promise. One of the most talented is midfield man Jean Tigana, who was outstanding in a home 3-2 win over Belgium. However, there are not enough good newcomers to give France long-term confidence in such an arduous competition. They should progress to the second phase of the finals from Group Four, which also contains England, Czechoslovakia and Kuwait.

Confidence was lacking especially before the win over Belgium in Paris. There had been a disturbing defeat in Holland and friendly games were lost. The early victories over Cyprus (7-0 in Limassol) and at home to the Republic of Ireland (2-0) did not signal the struggle ahead. In the end France qualified and at their best they are still an exciting side. Much depends on their making a good start and on their self-confidence.

Man of destiny: Michel Hidalgo, the French team manager, has not had an easy time guiding his side to the finals from a strong qualifying group. His experiments with new players and different formations have not always met with approval in France. Now he may hold England's fate in his hands, not to mention Czechoslovakia and Kuwait.

Man of alacrity: Dominique Rocheteau will be a prime French weapon in attack with his electrifying pace. He created the second goal in France's 2-0 win over Holland in Paris in November 1981 which clinched their place in the finals. He was not always available in the qualifying matches and missed the important game in Dublin.

THE SOVIET UNION

Colour: red shirts, white shorts (*reserve colours:* all white)

If there is to be a surprise in Spain, the Soviet Union must be a prime candidate. They finished their qualifying programme in Group Three unbeaten and caused a good Welsh team to be eliminated. Their 3-0 win over Wales in Tbilisi in November 1981 confirmed the return of a world class Soviet team.

After beating Wales, the Soviet record showed that in two years and 16 games they had not been beaten. Naturally, Wales had no great hopes of the Soviet side beating Czechoslovakia in Bratislava at the end of the qualifying programme. The Czechs needed only one point to finish above them. Sure enough, it was a draw.

Russian master: Konstantin Beskov is the team coach of the Soviet Union. He has welded a fine side from Dynamo Kiev, Dynamo Tbilisi and Moscow Spartak.

In the past, Soviet international teams have rarely been as good as their best club sides. The vast distances between major cities have always caused difficulties in producing a regular team of players with similar styles. There is a considerable difference between the character of a team from Moscow and another from Tbilisi in Georgia. At last it seems that a really exciting Soviet team has developed in time for the World Cup.

At the start of the qualifying matches manager Konstantin Beskov (also coach to Moscow Spartak) was attempting to draw on players from all over the Soviet Union, but later he concentrated on those from the big three clubs, Dynamo Tbilisi, Dynamo Kiev and Spartak. Before important international matches Beskov asks the players to write an unsigned note suggesting the team. Whether the selection panel take any notice is their secret.

With four qualifying games left to play, the Soviet Union suffered a blow when the skilful David Kipiani broke a leg, ironically when playing in Spain's Bernabeu Stadium. This elegant Dynamo Tbilisi player had been outstanding in his club's victory in the European Cup Winners' Cup. Then matters were made worse when Tengiz Sulakvelidze, another of Tbilisi's successful team, also missed matches because of injury. At the same time Kiev's Alexander Berezhnoi was banned for life, allegedly for persistent drunkenness.

For several years the Soviet Union's most consistent goalscorer, Oleg Blokhin of Dynamo Kiev, has been wooed by western European clubs. On the day when he scored two goals and had one disallowed against Turkey he was refused permission to join Real Madrid. The Soviet authorities are well aware of his value to their World Cup hopes. His goals against Turkey put the team on top of Group Three on goal difference. Blokhin, the son of Ukraine sprint champions, has scored more often than any

Above: White Russian: Vladimir Bessanov in the Soviet change strip (usually they play in red). He missed the last qualifying game against Wales, but will be a key player if fit.

Below: Soviet leader: Alexander Chivadze shows the destructive ability to beat opponents, which the Russians hope he can repeat in Spain.

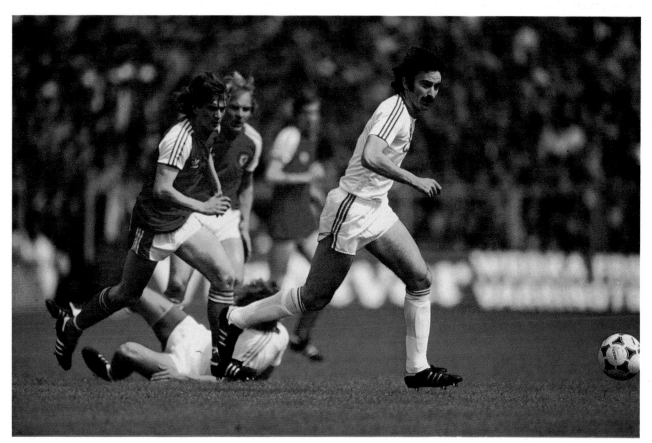

other Soviet player at club or international level.

The countries who visited the Soviet Union and returned without scoring complained about the frustrating delays and formalities. But the group's real losers, Wales, were in no position to argue with the manner of their defeat in Tbilisi.

Blokhin and the other top scorer, Shengelia, were unstoppable. Yet the Soviet side still lacked Kipiani, Chivadze and Bessonov. With all three fit again it will take an inspired and disciplined side to eliminate them in Spain. This is the task that faces Brazil, Scotland and New Zealand in Group Six.

Oleg Blokhin

European Footballer of the Year as long ago as 1975, Blokhin was still good enough to be voted fifth in 1981. At 29, this blond, natural left-winger has tremendous speed and a powerful left-foot shot. He is one of the world's most efficient scoring wingers. Until recently he was the only real star in Soviet football.

Born in Kiev, he was brought up in an athletics-minded family but joined the Kiev club and made his international debut in the 1972 Olympic team. His 153rd goal for the excellent Dynamo Kiev side made him the highest scorer in the history of Soviet club soccer. The record, previously held by Alexander Ponomaryov, had stood for 25 years. He is also the Soviet Union's leading marksman in internationals.

His remarkable record of international appearances has been achieved despite some brushes with Soviet football authority. Now married to the former world champion rhythmic gymnast Irina Deryugina, he seems settled and is playing as well as ever.

CZECHOSLOVAKIA

Czechoslovakia, who have been drawn in the same group as England in Spain, line up in 1980 (back row, left to right): Nehoda, Goegh, Kozak, Ondrus, Netolicka, Jerkemik and (front) Gajduskek, Vijek, Barmos, Panenka and Stambacher. The team was fairly stable during the qualifying competition and went through with the Soviet Union.

Colours: red shirts, white shorts (*reserve colours:* all white)

A point from their last match against the Soviet Union in November gave Czechoslovakia a place in Spain and prevented Wales from qualifying. Soon after winning the refreshing European Championship of 1976, they failed to qualify for Argentina. They will be especially keen to do well this time.

They began their defence of the European title with six of the team from four years before. Ondrus, Nehoda and Masny were among them and they reached the third place play-off with the hosts, Italy. On the way to that match they drew 1-1 with the Dutch. They then beat the Italians on penalties after a 1-1 draw. So they moved on to the World Cup qualifying competition reasonably confident and still playing their considered, short passing game.

The Czechs discovered that Wales were to be among their rivals. They had faced each other in previous championships and on meeting again in Cardiff there was little between them. Wales scored the only goal of the match early on but the Czechs should probably have had a penalty.

Against Turkey, Nehoda, winning his 70th cap, scored two goals to beat them at home. In the return the Czechs won 3-0 in Istanbul. They continued to keep the Soviet Union and Wales under pressure by beating Iceland 6-1. At that point Wales still led the group, despite dropping a point at home to the Soviet Union, but the Czechs had a game in hand.

A 4-0 win over a European XI in a special match to celebrate the Czech federation's 80th anniversary boosted confidence. Also it was good preparation for the crucial home game against Wales in September. Wales, then unbeaten, lost their buoyancy early in the game when Panenka's shot hit the post and rebounded in off Davies's arm. Nehoda, the only veteran, later set up Licka with a headed goal.

An uncomfortable 1-1 draw with Iceland put Czechoslovakia above Wales on goal difference but they could not be certain of qualifying with the Soviet Union for another two months. Wales helped the Czech cause by being held at home to a 2-2 draw by Iceland and by their defeat in the Soviet Union. The Czechs managed a 1-1 draw at home to the Soviet team who until then had conceded only one goal in seven games.

Aided by players with club experience in the west, Czechoslovakia (Olympic champions in Moscow) have a technically efficient team that is unlikely to make silly mistakes. Masny is still an accomplished ball player and Nehoda finishes strongly. Unfortunately, the central defender, Ondrus, captain of the 1976 European Championship side, has been in poor form after moving to Club Brugge and this may leave the Czech defence short of experience in Spain in Group Three.

Old campaigner: Nehoda won his 70th international cap for Czechoslovakia in their qualifying game at home to Turkey. He is a potent goalscorer and shows here that there is life left in the veteran body. He will be a menace to English, French and Kuwaiti defences. Czechoslovakia have not achieved much since they won the European Championship.

HUNGARY

Colours: red shirts, white shorts (*reserve colours:* all white)

Hungary have never quite rekindled the magic of the 1950s. They began badly in 1978 when two of their most skilful players, Tibor Nyilasi and Andras Torocsik, were sent off against the host nation. They were unable to recover and finished last in their group, having also lost to Italy and France. There has been some reorganization since then, though many of the 1978 squad remain, together with the doubts about consistency.

After Argentina, manager Lajos Baroti resigned and later Kalman Meszöly took over. The new man had to endure a World Cup qualifying group full of curious results and changing fortunes. Yet by the time he took Hungary to England for their last game, they had qualified. England still needed a point. Hungary's 1-0 defeat at Wembley was hardly a representative performance. Their effort was minimal.

They wanted to forget the demoralizing home defeat by England in June but they had to wait three months before meeting Romania in Bucharest. The result did little to prove that they could be an attacking force. By taking off Torocsik and Laszlo Kiss, both potential goalscorers, the Hungarians played for a dangerous goalless draw.

They reserved their best football for the next game against Switzerland in Budapest. They were without Gyozo Martos and Laszlo Balint, two foreign-based defenders who were suspended. Meszöly had to make careful plans. He brought in Sandor Müller for midfield work and filled the vacant defensive positions with Kerekes and Szanto. Sandor Sallai, a tenacious young midfield player, was given the task of marking the experienced Botteron.

The effect was surprisingly good. Hungary won 3-0 with Nyilasi scoring twice and then combining with Müller to give the veteran Laszlo Fazekas the third. Fazekas played his first game for the national team in 1968 but is still a regular scorer. Indeed, he added another goal when Hungary beat Norway 4-1 to qualify.

In the months before the finals, the Hungarians have been concerned about the fitness of Nyilasi, a brilliant player if fully fit and in the mood to show his skills. Injuries and stomach trouble kept him out of the last qualifying match against England. Without him they may lack ideas, but Torocsik could be one of the outstanding players of the finals – if he keeps his temper.

Above: pointing the way: Kalman Meszöly directs Hungary's affairs. He took over as team manager from Lajos Baroti after the 1978 finals.

Next page: eastern blockade: a tangle of East Europeans in the World Cup qualifying game between Hungary and Romania in September 1981.

Hungary cannot be compared with their great predecessors, nor do the younger members like the comparison. Their performance over the past 18 months has been erratic, but Meszöly has done well to ride through the crisis brought about by England's victory in Budapest.

The complications of the qualifying group were best summarized by the Norwegian manager, Tor Fossen, who said in October 1981: 'All we have to do is beat Hungary 3-0. Then if the Swiss defeat Romania 1-0 we are through, provided the match at Wembley does not end in a draw.'

ENGLAND

Colours: white shirts, blue shorts (*reserve colours:* red shirts, white shorts)

When the draw for the qualifying competition was made England found themselves in Group Four with Switzerland, Romania, Norway and Hungary. Even the most pessimistic critics conceded that the former world champions could hardly fail to reach the finals. In the event everything depended on the last match in November 1981 at Wembley. The Hungarians arrived having already qualified and England needed one point to join them in Spain.

England had made little impact on the European Championships in 1980. Kevin Keegan, on whom they relied for inspiration, seemed worn out by public expectancy and his own industry. Trevor Francis, who was expected to become the most exciting

Off to sunny Spain: Paul Mariner ends on his knees after scoring the only goal of England's match at Wembley against Hungary. This goal ensured that England qualified for the finals, although it was rather a lucky effort.

Bryan Robson

Few of England's players escaped criticism as the team scrambled into the finals. Even Kevin Keegan took his share. But Robson, a comparative newcomer, was superbly consistent. He and McDermott were the only players to appear in all eight of England's qualifying matches.

He was comfortable in international football, even in his first appearance for England in February 1980, but his path to the top was not completely smooth. Born in Chester-le-Street in County Durham, he became a fine youth player. He joined West Bromwich Albion and midlanders felt England were slow to realize his potential. He had won their admiration by his fighting recovery after breaking a leg three times in the 1976-77 season.

Manchester United could not be accused of under-estimating his value. They paid West Bromwich a record £1.7 millions to obtain his durable, dependable midfield skill. His style is thoroughly modern. He is a hard-working ball winner and thoughtful passer. He represents the very best of the English game.

Now firmly established in the England side, Robson is most valuable in midfield

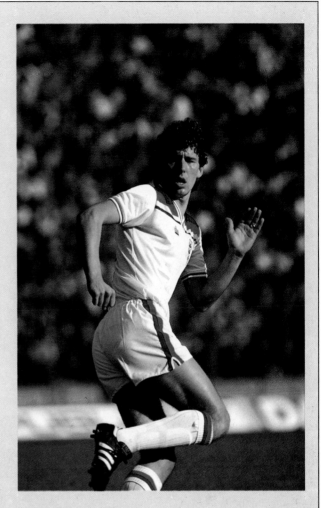

but he is flexible enough to have appeared in the centre of defence. Later in his career he may adopt this position.

finisher, was injured. The reign of the respected manager, Ron Greenwood, stumbled.

Though England began their World Cup qualifying series with a welcome but flattering 4-0 home win over Norway, the group was to be the strangest of all in Europe and for Greenwood it was a time of almost permanent concern.

After England had beaten the Norwegians without Keegan, Francis and Ray Wilkins, there was still a morbid feeling that no matter who Greenwood chose, the team would not be truly 'world class'. A 2-1 defeat in Romania the following month increased the doubts, although injuries again deprived Greenwood of several established

players including Keegan. The centre of defence was an area of particular difficulty.

In the meantime there had been a hint of the strange character of the group when the Norwegians recovered from their beating by England to secure a home 1-1 draw with Romania. Greenwood maintained his placid attitude by saying that it was a group in which points snatched by the Norwegians and the Swiss could be decisive. Hungary shrewdly arranged to hold their home games against Norway and Switzerland late in the competition when they hoped practice would have left them in good form. But Greenwood's forecast proved right.

Hungary, without Nyilasi, gave up a

point to Switzerland in a 2-2 draw whereas at Wembley England had beaten the Swiss 2-1. In the first half of that game England's teamwork was highly praised. Bryan Robson showed that he could act as a central defender and Trevor Brooking was the most sophisticated player on the field. Then the Swiss took a tighter hold and Steve Coppell was unable to find enough space on the wing. England faded. This tendency to lose momentum after beginning well remains one of their main problems.

A friendly match against Spain, again at Wembley, further exposed flaws. There was no criticism of the work but hard running did not make up for a lack of enterprise and Spain won 2-1. Towards the end of the winter England resumed their World Cup programme against Romania at Wembley. Keegan was absent, yet again, but the excuses were not enough for the crowds who saw Romania cling to a point. They jeered England from the field after a 0-0 draw. Only Robson, now a constant source of satisfaction, and the tireless Coppell, enhanced their reputations.

There followed a period of increasing depression. Although a weakened team restricted the visiting Brazilians to one goal from Zico, the home international tournament was a worrying prelude to the summer tour which was to include two World Cup games in Switzerland and Hungary. Their fifth home game without victory came when an injury-stricken Scotland won 1-0. Returning to the World Cup, they made terrible defensive mistakes in Switzerland at the end of May 1981, losing 2-1. Despite Keegan's return, the whole performance was discouraging.

So when they met Hungary in Budapest

Left: action man: Kevin Keegan has been in fine form for his club Southampton this season and he is among the leading goalscorers. England will need him in his sharpest form if they are to make any impact in Spain.

Below: goal-bound: Steve Coppell scores for England against Scotland in May 1979. Coppell is a tireless provider of ammunition for the England strikers, usually from the right. He is in the forefront of Greenwood's plans.

73

a week later morale was at its lowest point since Greenwood took over. He said: 'This is a game for character, attitude and experience.' Surprisingly, he chose an ageing team but for his sake as much as their own they did everything he asked. Admittedly the Hungarians were lax in their marking.

Brooking's well driven first goal early in the game, his dazzling second with a shot that lodged in the net and the reappearance of Thompson in the centre of defence were crucial factors. England won 3-1.

The sense of relief was tinged with doubt. England's best exhibition of the series had

Turning the tide

England's fortunes and morale were at their lowest ebb when they went to Budapest in June 1981. They had just been beaten in Switzerland and their chances of qualifying for the World Cup finals looked dim. Ron Greenwood relied on his most trusted and experienced players in this last-ditch effort to salvage national pride. Trevor Brooking was the star and scored twice in

England's 3-1 win. The brilliant goal illustrated above was the first of the match and lifted England's confidence. Steve Coppell found Kevin Keegan on the edge of the six-yard box. Keegan passed back to Brooking on the edge of the penalty area and the West Ham man rifled a great shot into the top corner. The ball lodged where it found the net in the goal frame.

been achieved with a team containing nine players who had appeared against Bulgaria as long ago as June 1979. Would Greenwood's loyalty, which was so well rewarded in Budapest, merely delay the arrival of younger players?

The next game, against Norway in Oslo in September 1981, revived the sense of despair. Again England began strongly, with Robson scoring after 15 minutes, but the Norwegians came into the game to score twice before half-time and win 2-1. England were left relying on the other countries to give them a helping hand by

Trevor Brooking

In the rush of a typical, hectic English league match Brooking seems to create his own time and space. Even in the exciting atmosphere of the West Ham ground his composure sets him apart.

The moves Brooking devises from midfield are often built on his powerful but easy-paced diagonal runs across the pitch. But the greatest skill of this big man (height: 6 ft ½in, weight: 13 st) is the well-timed, perceptive pass through the defence. In the England team he forms a partnership with Kevin Keegan who benefits from his shrewd passing. But Brooking is himself a talented scorer. His second goal against the Hungarians in the Nep Stadium was a classic. His goal against Arsenal won the FA Cup for West Ham in 1980.

Now Brooking is in his early thirties, Spain offers him one last chance to show a world-wide audience the delightful skills first cultivated by Ron Greenwood when he was West Ham's manager. Brooking joined West Ham from school and has remained with them. Injuries and doubts about his speed have cost him caps. He won his first for England in 1974 and has played more than 500 games for West Ham.

producing the right sequence of results. Later that month Romania and Hungary drew 0-0 in Bucharest. The result could not have been worse for England.

So while Hungary slipped quite comfortably into the finals, England just hoped Switzerland would help by restraining Romania, their challengers for the second qualifying place. It was a faint hope but the Swiss surpassed themselves. They won 2-1 in Bucharest and the Romanian manager was sacked. Switzerland and Romania played a goalless draw in Berne. Hungary had comfortable home wins over Switzerland and Norway, leaving England in need of only one point against the Hungarians at Wembley.

It would be misleading to claim that the 1-0 win England achieved over the Hungarians was in any way proof that they reached the finals on their own merit. Significantly Greenwood wore the Swiss tie on the day after qualifying. Beneath the immediate elation over Mariner's untidy winning goal was the knowledge that all too rarely the team played well enough to impress the rest of the world. At least Keegan seemed fit to last through to the finals and Robson continued to improve as an international, but the squad was lacking in reliable goalscorers. There was also the problem of finding cover for Watson, the long-serving central defender who was no longer in command of a regular place at club level. Alvin Martin was tried against Hungary but was hardly tested.

If the long, hard English club season – made longer by a hard winter and fixture chaos – leaves the squad without too many injuries, the team could progress through the first stages in Group Four in Bilbao. But to expect them to challenge the very best teams of the modern game would be to ignore their recent history. English football has never been in greater need of miracles.

Hokey-cokey: 'You put your left arm in' seems to be the message from England manager Ron Greenwood (*left*) to his

goalkeepers, Ray Clemence and Peter Shilton, who have taken it in turns to wear the yellow jersey for their country.

YUGOSLAVIA

Colours: blue shirts, white shorts (*reserve colours:* all white)

A country from which 200 or more players have departed to seek careers in foreign professional leagues can feel fortunate and a little surprised to be in the World Cup finals. Yugoslavia have reached Spain despite this steady exodus of their most experienced footballers and a crisis or two along the way.

Miljan Miljanic, the former Red Star Belgrade and Real Madrid manager, returned to Yugoslavia when the international team were beyond recovery in the European Championship preliminary competition. He rebuilt the side with younger players but soon became infuriated by the system. He felt that by allowing so many

older players to go abroad, especially to England and West Germany, the stability of the national side was being ruined. He threatened to leave but eventually persuaded the national federation to stop home-based members of his squad from moving abroad.

The irony of failing to qualify for the Championships was that immediately before the competition Yugoslavia could claim to be the most successful European team. From November 1979 to the summer of 1980 they had a run of nine victories.

Despite a disappointing Olympic Games, which they had hoped would prove their progress, the restored team began the qualifying round of the World Cup with a 5-0 win in Luxembourg. This softened the blow of the Balkan Cup defeat by Romania which

Veteran to the rescue: Dino Zoff, the veteran Italian goalkeeper, shows his usual courage by plunging at the feet of Yugoslavia's Halihodzic in the World Cup qualifying match in Belgrade in October 1981.

77

had ended their unbeaten record.

The 1980 Olympic campaign had brought them fourth place in a typically Eastern-dominated tournament. Then there was a crisis when they were about to play the Italians, potentially one of the World Cup favourites and considered the strongest side in the qualifying group. Miljanic was deprived of three injured players and then lost three more because of military service. He threatened to resign. Yugoslavia lost 2-0, only playing well when it was too late.

Miljanic was even more furious to discover that Buljan, one of the players who had been stopped from joining the team because he was allegedly unfit, in fact had scored a goal for Hamburg on the same day as the international match.

Three wins by Greece put Yugoslavia's position in doubt. They came face to face with the Greeks in Split in April 1981. They took a three-goal lead by half-time and finished 5-1 winners. One of their goals was a penalty taken by their goalkeeper, Pantelic, who is regularly seen running the length of the field to take the spot kicks.

They were then favourites to go to Spain with the criticized but still unbeaten Italians. Italy's vulnerability showed in a weary 2-0 home win against Denmark and they were exposed again by Yugoslavia in Belgrade. But for the goalkeeping of veteran Dino Zoff, Italy would have suffered a heavy defeat. Instead they escaped with a 1-1 draw. Yugoslavia were satisfied and completed their qualifying work by again beating Luxembourg 5-0.

When including their better exiles, Yugoslavia can be a tough, determined side. The proof of that came when winning 2-1 in Denmark where Italy had lost. Four foreign-based players, Pantelic, Halilhodzic, Slijvo and Surjak, contributed. In Spain, Miljanic expects that some of the team's best work will come from the fine home-based midfield player, Vladimir Petrovic, and also Safet Susic. Susic returned from national service for the last two qualifying matches and, though apparently slower, his ball control could trouble defences.

Master builder: Miljan Miljanic, the Yugoslav team manager, returned home to rebuild the national side when they were beyond recovery in the European Championship. He has managed Red Star Belgrade and Real Madrid.

ITALY

Colours: blue shirts, white shorts (*reserve colours;* white with blue stripes)

Nothing changes. Enzo Bearzot, the amazingly patient manager, goes to the finals being pilloried by his critics, just as he was four years ago. Italy were fourth in Argentina and in the European Championship.

Roberto Bettega

For years Italy's teams have been built around Juventus players. Bettega has been proof that manager Enzo Bearzot's policy is well founded. This strong but artistic striker has superb balance, is good in the air and has the speed of thought to overcome crunching Italian-style tackling.

He has scored some of Italy's finest and most important goals. In 1976 Bill Shankly, the witty and astute manager of Liverpool, described Bettega's diving header against England in Rome as among the greatest goals of the century.

Bettega was born in Turin 31 years ago. As a boy he watched Juventus from the terraces and there was never any doubt that he would join them. But he came to prominence, by scoring 13 goals in 30 games, in the 1969-70 season when loaned to the second division club Varese. He returned to Juventus and his goals helped take them to the championship.

His international career was cruelly delayed by severe lung trouble. In 1972 it seemed that he would have to give up football altogether. Doctors advised him to retire but he struggled back to fitness.

His international debut did not come until 1975. Once established, he became a regular and effective member of the attack. In the 1978 finals he scored the goal that caused Argentina's only defeat. These finals began well for him but ended poorly. He seemed jaded. Being a 'target man' in Italian football is a tiring business.

Golden boy thwarted: Antognoni, once the golden boy of Italy, has a crack at goal from a free kick in the third place play-off in 1978. This effort was saved by Leao, the Brazilian goalkeeper, and Brazil came from behind to win the match 2-1 in Buenos Aires.

They dearly want to become the first European team to win the World Cup three times. Their last victory was 44 years ago.

In Spain they could survive Group One against Peru, Poland and Cameroon. But in the second phase they will have to be at their sharpest to overcome Argentina and the Soviet Union (or Scotland).

Italy have not been helped by their bribery scandals and the resulting suspension of the gifted Paolo Rossi. His absence cost them more than they would admit. During and even before the qualifying matches Bearzot was nervous about the outcome.

The manager was even more troubled after the opening game in Luxembourg. He almost resigned. Italy won 2-0, with goals from Collovati and Bettega, but for a time they seemed in real danger of conceding a lead if not losing the match. Causio and Antognoni were sent off and suspended from the next game against Denmark in Rome but the Danes were easily beaten and this time Bearzot's concern was misplaced

since Graziani gave Italy the lead after only seven minutes. The unusual feature of the game was Bettega's appearance in midfield.

Antognoni reappeared against Yugoslavia and Bruno Conti, a little winger who had waited a long time for international recognition, scored after beating several defenders. Italy won 2-0. They went to Uruguay for the Gold Cup tournament but met the hosts in a rough game in which only Antognoni was prepared to risk running with the ball. Italy lost 2-0 and Bearzot said the match was an affront to football.

Without Benetti, the hard midfield man of the 1978 team, Italy have found it difficult to take a firm hold of matches. They lost their unbeaten record in the group in Denmark. Bettega said the 3-1 defeat could

Eyes down: everybody's attention is fixed on a duel between Stefanson, the Romanian no. 5, and Cabrini of Italy during the match between the two countries in 1980. Cabrini's club, Juventus, also provides Zoff, Tardelli and Bettega.

be blamed on the tiredness of the players but the supporters were again unmoved. Bearzot remarked that if Denmark could always show such teamwork they would be world beaters.

A comparatively new midfield player, Giuseppe Dossena, appeared in a more hopeful friendly 3-2 win in Bulgaria. He was retained for the World Cup game against Yugoslavia in Belgrade where 39-year-old Zoff prevented an embarrassing defeat.

Conti continued to make a good impression as Italy guaranteed their place in Spain by drawing 1-1 with Greece in Turin, but the team were without Bettega and Rossi in attack and Tardelli in midfield and failed to convince a critical crowd.

The Greeks organized their defence effectively. They equalized three minutes from the end after a misunderstanding in the Italian defence. Kouis's header beat Zoff who was making a record 95th appearance in goal for Italy. Yet even when they had been released from the worry of qualifying, Italy could not unwind. Their last home game against Luxembourg produced a disappointing 1-0 win against a team who had already conceded 22 goals.

As they entered World Cup year itself, Italy still awaited confirmation that Rossi would be ready to play when his suspension ended in April. They were also concerned that former golden boy Antognoni had not fully recovered from a fractured skull suffered in a tough league match. After a collision with a goalkeeper he had to be saved by the kiss of life.

Next page: moment of joy: Italy have scored through Causio in the 1978 third place play-off against Brazil. Causio is buried by joyous team mates because he has given his side the lead. But Brazil went on to win the match. The Italian in the no. 21 shirt is Rossi who has been banned for corruption and could miss the 1982 finals.

81

SCOTLAND

Colours: blue shirts, white shorts (*reserve colours:* white shirts, blue shorts)

Haunted by memories of failure in Argentina and a habit of falling below their potential, Scotland know that they should approach Spain more realistically. Team manager Jock Stein has done his best to quieten the euphoria of qualifying from Group Six. But he is aware that the dedicated fans would walk to the ends of the earth to follow the team and cannot be subdued.

Scotland failed to qualify for the European Championship and needed a solid start in a World Cup group containing Portugal, Northern Ireland, Sweden and Israel (a late addition by FIFA who wanted to avoid placing them in a group with Arab countries for political reasons).

The Scots went first to Sweden and won

1-0. Gordon Strachan, one of the young lions in midfield, scored from a move created by Archie Gemmill, one of the veterans. The overall performance was merely adequate. There was a need to build team confidence among a group of such talented forwards as Kenny Dalglish, Andy Gray, John Robertson, and occasionally Joe Jordan, now based in Milan. They had the responsibility of completing the work done by equally gifted midfield players and such composed defenders as Alan Hansen and Danny McGrain.

Doubts about the defence as a unit persisted well into the qualifying competition, yet in five games no goals were allowed to pass. There are goalkeeping worries.

The first serious test came with a visit

'We'll support you evermore': Scottish banners unfurl as their fans put on a typical display of passion. This great weight of expectation can be a handicap as well as a help.

Asa Hartford

Early in 1981 Hartford was struggling for a place in the Everton team and could not get in the Scottish side. By the end of the year he was captain of Manchester City and Scotland and fighting back with a defiance often seen before in his varied career.

This stocky, driving force of Scotland's midfield is far from being one of the young hopefuls looking for stardom in Spain. Now 31, he has suffered more disappointments than most, not least in Argentina. The low point of his career came in 1971 when his £171,000 transfer from West Bromwich Albion to Leeds United was called off because doctors discovered he had a 'hole in the heart'. He went back to West Bromwich and after medical clearance proved he had the heart to succeed.

Manchester City bought him for the first time in 1974. After five years' service for City and Scotland he was transferred to Nottingham Forest where he hardly had time to get to know the management team of Brian Clough and Peter Taylor before being sold. He joined Everton but his career seemed over when he lost his place in their team.

A return to Manchester City in 1981 revived his spirits. His reappearance in the Scottish side has coincided with their more solid, dependable style of play. He admits that teams like West Germany 'are in a different league' but his determination is one of the reasons why Scotland go to Spain looking a more practical team than in 1978.

from Portugal. Only the previous spring the Portuguese had lost 4-1 at Hampden Park in a European Championship qualifying game. They were desperately keen not to miss out on the World Cup. Portugal played defensively and Gray and Dalglish could not break them down. The result was a dispiriting goalless draw. Fears were spreading that Dalglish had lost his scoring touch.

A visit to Israel created more problems than Scotland had expected but, despite suffering double vision, Dalglish did score against a side who had compiled three draws against Northern Ireland, and Sweden (twice) and beaten the Austrians in a friendly. Israel were far from a makeweight in the group and ended with a much improved reputation, as well as one remarkable 4-1 victory over Portugal.

Dalglish was missing from the home match against Northern Ireland but it was the defenders who caused the most concern. The Irish worried them after taking the lead with 20 minutes left. Although the powerful John Wark equalized, the midfield players were not omitted from Stein's sharp criticism.

When Israel went to Hampden Park they also bothered the Scotland defence, but not for long. The prize of Spain came nearer with a 3-1 win. Jordan was called up from

Italy for the match with Sweden and opened the scoring in the 2-1 victory. The Swedes were unfortunate to lose so many points early in the qualifying games. Their football in the second half of 1981 was such that on this form they deserved to be among the finalists as they had been in the previous two World Cups.

Against Northern Ireland, Scotland needed one point to qualify. The Irish still had hopes of qualifying themselves. Scotland were undefeated and on the verge of being the first of the British teams to be among the final 24. Apart from Jordan, who was absent, the team now had cohesion and a goalless draw gave Scotland the required point.

Stein had tried hard to keep a sense of proportion, but remarked that it was pleasing to reach Spain without the help of favourable results from other countries. Later Scotland lost their unbeaten record in the last qualifying game in Portugal, but by then their thoughts were in Spain.

In a year Scotland had lost only one game in ten and Stein had developed a squad strong enough to give confidence of success in the finals. Perhaps they rarely showed the glimpses of delightful enterprise seen in previous Scotland teams, but they approached their third successive World Cup finals in a much more practical frame of mind. They hope that Dalglish will recover his most devastating finishing form and that the defence will not revert to the faults of the past. So they are unlucky to be drawn in one of the toughest groups in the finals, with Brazil and the Soviet Union.

In midfield they have gained from Asa Hartford's considered football and the power of Souness. Overall they are better prepared than four years ago, but, as Stein says, Scotland is still a small country. The supporters will not see it that way.

Power player: Graeme Souness shows his strength as he leaves Yorath of Wales trailing in his wake. Scotland made the mistake of leaving out Souness in 1978 until their cause was almost lost. He has been one of the vital cogs in the Liverpool machine and will undoubtedly figure in Jock Stein's midfield plans.

NORTHERN IRELAND

Colours: green shirts, white shorts (*reserve colours:* white shirts, green shorts)

A troubled country of fewer than two million people, Northern Ireland still regularly produce outstanding footballers who usually move to the English league. Only occasionally do they create a national team to reach the heights in world football. The last and only time they qualified for the World Cup finals was in 1958.

One of the secrets of their appearance in Spain is the arrival of their manager Billy Bingham, a member of that 1958 team. Unlike previous managers, he has a pragmatic approach. Like any ambitious club manager he began organizing the Irish team by improving the defence.

Northern Ireland's opening game in Group Six shed no light on their chances. Indeed, light itself was scarce in Tel-Aviv where the Irish had to be satisfied with a 0-0 draw with Israel under fading floodlights. Pat Jennings, their veteran but still remarkably agile goalkeeper, had an outstanding game.

Jim Platt deputized efficiently when Jennings missed Northern Ireland's game against Sweden in Belfast. Sammy McIlroy was one of the scorers in their 3-0 victory and he became the team's most important figure. His skill in midfield became a shining light at times when others seemed to run blindly. Sweden had recently provided a European Cup final team, Malmö, and were highly experienced World Cup

Irish out of luck: Chris Nicholl defends for Northern Ireland in their sad defeat in Sweden. Jimmy Nicholl gave away a penalty and was sent off with Sweden's Borg after they had come to blows. This setback to the Irish was reversed when the Portuguese challenge faded in later qualifying games. Portugal were quickly defeated by Sweden.

travellers, so the result gave Northern Ireland some hope of a World Cup place.

Against Portugal in Lisbon, Gerry Armstrong, the powerful forward, had his nose broken, and several other players were badly bruised as the Portuguese took a 1-0 victory. But World Cup hopes returned in a rewarding 1-1 draw with Scotland in Glasgow. Bingham now knew he had to organize a victory over the Portuguese in

Pat Jennings

In the English league there is no shortage of great goalkeepers. Jennings is still one of the best at 36. Exactly six feet tall and with huge hands that grasp the ball with complete safety, he has vied with Ray Clemence and Peter Shilton for the title 'best goalkeeper in Britain'.

He has been Northern Ireland's first choice for 17 seasons. Since crossing the Irish sea to join Watford he has been a model of consistency. If he makes an error it becomes headline news.

Although he can be dominating in the thick of a crowded penalty area, he is by nature a quiet, courteous man. He commands his area of the pitch by speed off the line and by using his broad frame to block the paths of oncoming forwards.

His career began at Newry Town. Gaelic football had helped his handling but it was never his favourite game. After making the grade professionally with Watford he spent two years at Tottenham trying to make the first team goalkeeper's spot his own. When he succeeded he soon won the affection of the crowd.

He spent 13 years at White Hart Lane before Spurs let him go to Arsenal for a bargain £45,000. Despite several nasty injuries he has maintained his high standards and while other players of his age think of retirement he looks forward to his first World Cup finals.

Belfast. He expected a blanket defence and was almost right. But Armstrong headed a clever goal and the Irish were satisfied. A bottle was thrown on to the pitch and the Portuguese manager complained that this incident had destroyed his team's concentration.

Everything seemed favourable as the Irish went to Sweden. The Swedes had not won at home for 18 months and were still awaiting their first victory in the group. Their record of appearances in the finals was in danger. The only worry for Northern Ireland was that, because England had pulled out of a British championship match, they were short of practice.

Suddenly everything went wrong. Jimmy Nicholl gave away a penalty from which Borg scored the winning goal. Then Terry Cochrane exchanged blows with Borg and they were both sent off. At the end of a sad day the Irish had only an outside chance of qualifying. Three weeks later Sweden offered Ireland some compensation and themselves hope by beating Portugal.

Although Northern Ireland's next opponents, Scotland, needed only a point to qualify, a draw would probably not be enough for Northern Ireland. Bingham said it was essential to win the home games but Scotland got their point without having to score. The Russian referee refused appeals for a penalty and the Irish were left hoping that the other countries would offer a lifeline.

Portugal's challenge collapsed in their astonishing 4-1 defeat in Israel, leaving Northern Ireland in need of one point from their own second meeting with the Israeli side, this time in Belfast. Although the captain, Martin O'Neill, failed a fitness test, the Irish won with a low left foot drive from Armstrong.

While Northern Ireland may not concede many goals in Spain, their chances of being among the teams competing for the ultimate honour are remote. First they must eliminate their hosts or Yugoslavia in Group Five. Merely being there may help stimulate a people in need of hope.

POLAND

Colours: white shirts, red shorts (*reserve colours:* red shirts, white shorts)

With three countries in Group Seven, only one could qualify and Malta had no serious chance. East Germany and Poland were the contenders and the Poles won both matches. East Germany's manager, Georg Buschner, promptly resigned and Poland went to their third World Cup finals in succession. At a time of so much hardship in Poland, the success of the national team was timely. The new manager, Antoni Piechniczek, became a hero on the day they beat East Germany 3-2 in Leipzig.

Poland still rely on at least three of the players who assisted them in the finals of 1974 and 1978. Lato, who is in his thirties, was the highest scorer in the 1974 finals with seven goals but now he often works in midfield, providing chances for others. Zmuda, the 'libero', has more than 70 caps, and Szarmach, now playing in France, is still scoring goals. Lato and Szarmach were not released by their foreign clubs when Poland visited Argentina on a tour and won 2-1. Buncol and Boniek, back after suspension, scored the goals which encouraged the Poles in their preparations.

Among the younger players Poland hope to see develop in the finals is Wlodek Smolarek, who scored twice in Leipzig, and central defender Tadeusz Dolny.

The familiar face of goalkeeper Jan Tomaszewski is no longer certain of appearing. Now based in Spain, his local knowledge will be useful but his place in the side cannot be guaranteed. He will long be remembered in England where in 1973 his saves prevented the English from qualifying for the finals the following year.

In the World Cup in Argentina Poland were a little unfortunate being involved in what is now by tradition a goalless opening game, this one with West Germany. Later they lost 2-0 to the bubbling Argentines. They played bravely but made errors and Kazimierz Deyna, their captain who was playing his 100th international, even missed a penalty.

The Poles' first qualifying game for Spain was highly controversial. Even before leaving for Malta, Josef Mlynarczyk, one of their goalkeepers, was told to abandon the trip for being drunk. Some other players protested and he was allowed to travel but only as far as Rome. After more arguments, he and three others – including Boniek and Zmuda – were ordered home.

Troubles continued into the match itself. In the second half, with Poland leading 1-0 from a Smolarek goal, Lipka put the ball into the net. The Yugoslav referee overruled a linesman who flagged Lipka offside. When the crowd realized the goal was to stand they hurled stones. The referee abandoned the match and the score (2-0) remained in the records.

Later Mlynarczyk and Zmuda were suspended for eight months and Boniek and Terlecki for a year. Ryszard Kulesza, the manager at the time, said the sentences were too severe and he was sacked, leaving Piechniczek in charge.

Piechniczek brought in the veteran exiles Tomaszewski, Szarmach and Lato for the home game against East Germany. Ironically, the newcomer, Buncol, scored the winning goal. Boniek and Mlynarczyk were both restored to the team for the return game in East Germany.

In Spain with eight of the excellent 1974 team still available for the squad, Poland will be one of the more experienced sides. However, all the problems of the past months may not allow normal preparation.

Bald eagle: Lato, now in his thirties, was a Polish star in 1974, when Poland knocked out England and finished third in the finals. He appeared again in Argentina.

BRAZIL

Colours: yellow shirts, blue shorts (*reserve colours:* blue shirts, white shorts)

World Cup winners in 1958, 1962 and 1970 and the first country to qualify for 1982, Brazil are again the South American favourites. The country produces so many exceptional players that it is easy to understand why there is so much frustration when the national team fail to fulfil their potential. But they went sweetly to Spain from South American Group One with a 100 per cent record against Bolivia and Venezuela.

Since 1970 there has been a lot of heart searching. In 1974 Brazil were only fourth, and third in 1978. Although some of their football was skilful they were more physical than usual. Under their latest coach, Tele Santana, they have another team of great skill and style.

The Gold Cup tournament in Uruguay in 1981 was taken far more seriously by the South Americans than the Europeans, so the match between the World Cup holders, Argentina, and the Brazilians was significant. It ended in a draw and a large scale brawl but also contained brilliant football.

In the final, Brazil again confounded the 'purists' by playing the better football but losing 2-1 to Uruguay. They employed the familiar curling free-kicks, now performed by Junior, the thrusting, sudden attacks (encouraged from midfield by Socrates), and the wingmanship of Ze Sergio. With Isidoro dominating midfield, they should have kept control of the game.

While the outside world talks of Brazil as

Gold Cup losers: the Brazilians who lost to Uruguay in the 1981 final included: (back, left to right) Edevaldo, Toninho Cerezo, Oscar, Carlos Luizinho, Junior and (front) Jack (masseur), Tita, Renato, Socrates, Batista and Ze Sergio.

Zico

Brazil are always looking for a new Pelé. Many a promising young player has suffered from too much publicity too early. Zico was one of them. He also had a succession of injuries, but, at 29, he competes with Argentina's Maradona for the title 'best player in the world'.

Zico has been runner-up to Maradona as South America's Player of the year but there is little comparison between them. Zico is taller and looks more athletic. His art is timing. He splits defences with passes, stuns goalkeepers with snap shots or glides out of midfield into scoring positions. As a 'play-maker' or goalscorer he is invaluable to Brazil.

He won his first cap against Uruguay in 1976 but injuries have restricted his international appearances. He was not fit for the Gold Cup tournament in Uruguay and he might have made a better impression in the 1978 World Cup if Brazil had not tried to play a physical game. But in the past two years he has become the outstanding member of a Brazilian team, echoing the style of Pelé's hey-day.

In 1980 he was leading scorer in the Brazilian league with 21 goals in 18 games. Examples abound of his prodigious goal-scoring and goal-making. In Flamengo's world Club Cup match against Liverpool in Tokyo in December 1981 Zico was in splendid form. He appeared not to hurry yet he made the European champions seem cumbersome.

His most memorable goal-scoring feats include four against an Irish XI and four for Flamengo in their three-legged Libertadores Cup final against Cobreloa, of Chile, who thought they could mark him out of the game. He collected all three goals when Brazil beat Bolivia 3-1 to become the first country to qualify for the finals.

the best team going to Spain, Santana still expresses doubts about the quality of the younger players. An extraordinary 3-2 defeat by Qatar in the World Youth Cup may have led him to that conclusion. He remarked that it was fortunate that he was already sure of the players he would need for the World Cup. The Gold Cup and a tour of Europe, on which they beat West Germany 2-1, France 3-1, and England 1-0, confirmed his thoughts on team selection. He was not keen to recall players from Europe and should not need them.

Brazil under Santana are returning to the character of their finest teams, built on freedom of expression. Not long ago they moved towards a stronger style, but Santana says that in Spain the world will see the soccer everyone expects from Brazil. That warning should chill the hearts of their Group Six rivals.

While in Europe they indicated how far they had moved away from the hard, physical version of the game so resented by their fans at home and abroad. Against England at Wembley, Socrates and the winger, Eder, began by toying with the home defenders and Reinaldo swept cutting passes to Zico.

Santana's popularity was not easily won. His first five matches were unimpressive but in the past year Brazil have beaten all of the teams expected to do well in Spain, including the hosts, and the majority of the best players appear to be in fine form. Zico, who had previously suffered by comparisons with Pelé, began to look a marvellous player in his own right. He will surely be one of the oustanding entertainers in Spain.

Santana's idea of the best Brazilian squad may include Edevaldo, Oscar, Luisinho and Junior at the back, Socrates, Zico and Toninho Cerezo in midfield and Paulo Isidor, Roberto and Ze Sergio in attack. Eder and Falcao must also be considered.

When accepting the position as manager, Santana said: 'It is a good way to grow old quickly.' He knows that the Brazilian supporters cannot abide thoughts of failure.

Above: destination unknown: Reinaldo seemed to know where he was going in Brazil's 1-0 victory over England in May 1981. But now he is not so sure of his place in the side.

What's in a name: Socrates can play more like an executioner than the Greek philosopher with whom he shares his name. He showed some devastating style in May 1981 when he began by toying with the England defence. He could line up in the Brazilian midfield against Scotland in Group Six.

PERU

Colours: all white (*reserve colours:* red shirts, white shorts)

Uruguay, the first possessors of the World Cup and only last year winners of the Gold Cup tournament in their own country, will not be in Spain. Instead, Peru, an ageing team coached by Elba de Padua Lima, better known as 'Tim', qualified for Spain.

'Tim' is variously reported as being 63 or 71. 'The Professor', as he is also known, took over the team only two months before the start of the South American group competition, also containing the more favoured Uruguayans and Colombia. He worked wonders. Peru finished unbeaten.

Confidence barely existed before the opening games in Group Two. Preceding friendly matches had been unimpressive and so some of the older foreign exiles had to be recalled. Cubillas, in his early thirties, was summoned from the Fort Lauderdale Strikers. Cesar Cueto returned from Colombia. Oblitas rejoined them from

Belgium and the 38-year-old Chumpitaz was talked out of plans to retire. When he took his place in the centre of the defence the average age rose to over 27.

Playing composed and unusually slow football, they beat Uruguay 2-1 in Montevideo in the crucial game of the group and drew 0-0 at home. The conclusion was that skill, despite advanced years, could overcome intimidation.

Chumpitaz, who was a member of the 1970 World Cup team, is an essential contributor in defence. So far his position in the team has not been challenged by younger men. Behind him, in goal, remains Quiroga, the Argentine-born player nicknamed 'El Loco' who in 1978 was at the centre of a smear campaign when Argentina beat Peru 6-0.

'Tim' has so improved the team's organization and spirit that he feels 'we can

Peruvian goal-mine: La Rosa is a leading goalscorer for Peru. He relies greatly on speed and so does the rest of the attack which is bound to unsettle defences.

surprise the world even though nobody gave a cent for our chances when we started'. He is slightly concerned that there is no obvious cover for Chumpitaz who began the year with an achilles tendon injury.

One of the faults of the past was the frustrating tendency for the forwards to play unnecessary final passes as they ran into the opposition's penalty area. 'Tim' seems to have overcome the problem with La Rosa receiving good, speedy service from the wingers, Barbadillo (on the right) and Oblitas (on the left).

Speed has always been the key strength of Peru. In Spain they will again hope to

'All goalkeepers are mad': but few are as eccentric as the Peruvian goalkeeper Quiroga. Nicknamed 'El Loco', he was booked in 1978 for a rugby tackle in his opponent's half.

succeed through rapid breakaways. The acceleration of Cueto and Velasquez in midfield is likely to upset even the best defences and La Rosa's good goalscoring record is also based on pace. Cubillas is well remembered for his quick, skilful finishing but he is no longer sure of a place.

Without doubt Peru will be one of the most entertaining teams in Spain, but 'Tim's' claim that all the other nations will be afraid of them may be stretching optimism too far.

CHILE

Colours: red shirts, blue shorts (*reserve colours:* all white)

By finishing their South American Group

Three qualifying games against Ecuador and Paraguay with an unbeaten record and without conceding a single goal, Chile seemed to have a remarkable team. The

Flying winger: the 20-year-old Yanez in the red shirt demonstrates some of his pace in a game against Ecuador in June 1981. He will be a player to watch.

serious doubts about their chances in Spain, where they come up against West Germany, Austria and Algeria, concern their inexperience in playing against European opponents and their poor showing in five previous finals.

Methodically coached by the somewhat pessimistic Luis Santibañez, they are a side of strong defensive qualities. Although not to be compared with the Argentina of four years ago, their style is similar. The Argentina manager, Cesar Menotti, is a close friend of Santibañez and in 1980 their teams drew.

They are expected to play a counter-attacking game with Elias Figueroa, the 34-year-old three times South American Footballer of the Year, making most of the important decisions. The midfield section could be a weak link.

Santibañez says: 'I don't think we can play a starring role in Spain'. Yet Chile beat Paraguay, the South American champions, comfortably enough and after qualifying went to Rio de Janeiro with a weakened team and drew 0-0 with Brazil. They have also seen a revival in domestic football with Cobreloa, the 1981 league champions, reaching the final of the Libertadores Cup, the South American club competition.

Santibañez included no fewer than seven members of the Cobreloa team in his original World Cup squad: Wirth, Jiminez, Tabilo, Alarcon, Puebla, Soto and Escobar. But the expected star of the team is Patricio Yanez who plays for San Luis.

Yanez is a 20-year-old winger who has a thirst for goals. Several clubs in Chile have made offers to sign him but all were put off by a high asking price. If he has a good World Cup more offers will come, but this time from Europe.

Figueroa regularly commutes between Santiago, where he is involved in business, and Florida, where he plays for the Fort Lauderdale Strikers. His wide experience can be added to that of another veteran, Carlos Caszely.

Individual experience is highly valuable to any team but Chile as a unit may find that competition in Spain is too intense. Santibañez remained pessimistic even after his team had qualified. He confessed: 'I do not feel we are up to world standard.' They will need to be in better spirits if they are to achieve anything in Group Two against West Germany, Austria and Algeria.

ALGERIA

Colours: red and white shirts, red shorts (*reserve colours:* green and white)

This will be the first World Cup appearance for Algeria. Their journey has been hard and their supporters have sometimes endured much to see their team. If Algeria continue to progress, this side could spring some surprises in Spain.

Algeria came from a huge group of African teams all striving to do even better than Tunisia who beat Mexico and drew with the West Germans in 1978. The last eight countries left in the African qualifying competition for Spain were Algeria, Cameroon, Egypt, Guinea, Morocco, Nigeria, Niger and Zaire. Of those, Nigeria were the favourites to qualify. They were the African champions, having beaten Algeria 3-0 in the Cup of Unity, and had two outstanding players from the English league, John Chiedozie and Tunji Banjo.

Oil money gave Nigeria big advantages,

Zidane of Algeria is confronted by two Nigerians. The action comes from the second leg of their World Cup qualifier in Constantine where Algeria won 2-1.

including a trip to Brazil, but Algeria provided the surprise. They had done well in the Moscow Olympics, drawing 1-1 with Spain, beating Syria 3-0 and losing to the East Germans 1-0 before Yugoslavia beat them by 3-0 in the quarter-finals.

They confronted Nigeria in the fourth round of the World Cup qualifying competition. The first leg was in Lagos where their Russian coach, Yevgeni Rogov, caused a surprise by dropping two of the many French-based players, Dahleb and Djaadaoui. He was convinced that Lakhdar Belloumi, described as a mixture of Maradona and Platini, would win the game for him. He was right. Belloumi made an astonishing 40-yard run to score the first goal and set up Zidane for the second.

For the return leg in Constantine thousands of Algerians camped out all night to be sure of getting into the stadium. Although Nigeria were defiant and gave a better performance than in the first leg, they could not cope with Belloumi who again scored an opening goal. Algeria won 2-1 (4-1 on aggregate) to qualify.

Their strength is based on experience of playing sides from the Mediterranean countries and the help given by the Soviets. For the finals they are likely to have as many as six French-based players involved.

CAMEROON

Colours: green shirts, red shorts (*reserve colours:* yellow shirts, green shorts)

For the first time Africa is to be represented in the finals by two teams. Whether the 'Untameable Lions' from Cameroon can justify the opportunity is one of the more pertinent questions to be answered in the contentiously expanded competition.

Their chance comes as a result of beating the more favoured Morocco 4-1 on aggregate in the African group finals. Morocco were far more experienced internationally.

With a blend of their own amateur players and professionals from France and the United States, the national side are beginning to exploit the improvements seen at club level. Players from the Canon of Yaounde club are always prominent in a national squad coached by Branko Zutic, a Yugoslav appointed in 1980.

In the opening rounds of the African group they beat Malawi and Zimbabwe and then faced Zaire in the third round. Zaire had beaten them in the 1974 preliminary competition but this time Cameroon recovered from a 1-0 first leg defeat in Zaire to win the second 6-1.

At the outset few people gave them a

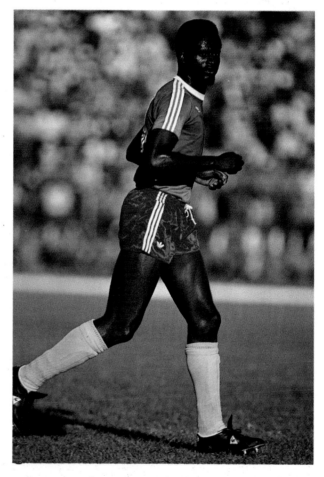

Abega, the Cameroon midfield player, is a likely starter in Spain. He plays for the Canon Club of Yaounde.

Kunde, another Cameroon
midfield player from the
Canon Club. He is 23 and
scored twice in
Cameroon's 3-0 home win
over Zurich in December
1981.

African King; the muscular
Roger Milla is the
undoubted star of the
Cameroon side. He plays
for Bastia in the French
league. But he and his
colleagues will do
extremely well to avoid
heavy defeats in Spain.
They will hope to be more
than cannon-fodder for
Italy, Poland and
Peru in Group One.

chance of success. The strength of the nation's football seemed too localized. During the qualifying games an understanding was developed and, even if against the better European and South American sides in Spain they may be outplayed tactically, their individuals will be interesting.

The undoubted 'star' of the side is the muscular Roger Milla who plays for Bastia in the French league, but they often have to rely on the goalkeeping of N'Kono who has the reputation of being the best goalkeeper ever produced by Africa.

One of the most consistent goalscorers at club and international level is Manga Onguene, of the Canon of Yaounde club. He was the African 'Footballer of the Year' in 1980, having scored nine goals during the African Cup of Champion Clubs. In his mid-thirties, he has played more than 60 times for Cameroon.

Cameroon will do well to avoid heavy defeats in Spain by Italy, Peru and Poland. For the sake of African soccer they need to show that the gap in ability between that continent and the established football nations is still closing.

EL SALVADOR AND HONDURAS

Toast of Honduras: Ramon Maradiaga, the Honduras captain, is highly popular at home. His face has been ravaged by illness and he is nicknamed 'El Primitivo', which is said to have nothing to do with his style of play.

Honduras colours: blue shirts, white shorts (*reserve colours:* all white)

El Salvador colours: all blue (*reserve colours:* all white)

Central America breathed a sigh of relief when the republics of Honduras and El Salvador both qualified. In 1969 El Salvador beat Honduras to qualify for the final tournament in Mexico the following year. The ensuing riot aggravated existing tension and led to war.

This time they go to Spain as joint representatives of the awkwardly named CONCACAF group which included countries belonging to the North and Central American and Caribbean confederation. Among the earliest victims, when the competition was still being played in regional zones, were the United States, who had high hopes of showing a sceptical world that they were making progress internationally.

Despite the growth in popularity of soccer in the United States, the country's massive infusion of foreign players is a mixed blessing. The national team of home-grown footballers won only one match in the Northern zone qualifying group from which Canada emerged to be

Above: happy as sandboys: Honduras have a holiday look about them as they pose for a picture during training. They were unbeaten in their play-offs, having spent 10 months training together rather than playing for their club teams.

Salvador Bernadez, a 26-year-old striker for Honduras. He had a stomach operation in the summer of 1981 but is expected to be in the squad for Spain.

Blue is the colour . . . for El Salvador who will be rank outsiders in Spain but here outnumber Mexico in a friendly in 1980.

one of six countries involved in a play-off in Honduras.

The Canadians had long since stopped relying almost entirely on visiting Europeans. In 1980, for instance, their national side consisted entirely of players born in the country or Europeans who had lived there since childhood. Obviously, the large post-war immigration of Italians was a big influence on the growth of the game in Canada.

Coached by former English schoolteacher and Derby County player Barrie Clarke, Canada expected to qualify along with Mexico. They included players with North American Soccer League experience but they were disappointing in the play-off. Even so, they would have gone to Spain had they beaten Cuba in their last match.

Honduras took full advantage of the con-troversial decision to hold all the play-off games in their country, but El Salvador were defensive and almost failed. Diplomacy between the countries reached a new peak when Honduras helped guarantee their neighbours a place in the finals by drawing with them and with Mexico. The Mexicans had appeared in eight of the previous 11 final competitions and, not surprisingly, were afraid to go home after El Salvador qualified.

Honduras finished the play-off tournament as comfortable, unbeaten winners. They had spent 10 months in training together rather than playing for their clubs. They became a strong, efficient team.

They are led by Ramon Maradiaga, a midfield player whose nickname, 'El Primitivo', is not entirely misleading. According to thousands of their supporters his nickname has nothing to do with the way he plays. They say it was first given him as a child when a priest saw him playing soccer

103

outdoors during a monsoon.

Maradiaga is the 24-year-old captain. He is so popular that during the first presidential elections for ten years he still captured the headlines and was mobbed in the streets. Yet his salary was only £150 a month – all his club, Motagua, could afford.

In Spain Maradiaga will be a menacing figure. A skin disease has left him with scars on his face and he looks much older than his years. Not that his football is without grace. His distribution was a source of goals in the qualifiers.

El Salvador are reputedly even tougher than Honduras. Their background makes that a credible threat. With the country in turmoil, the players have not been spared. One of them was killed by guerrillas, another died in crossfire and three others had relatives murdered. Resilience will not be enough in a finals group that also contains Argentina, Belgium and Hungary.

El Salvador's previous World Cup experience could be an asset but Honduras have probably made more progress, albeit aided by the fact that the play-off competition in the group took place in their own capital of Tegucigalpa where spectators waited at dawn for matches kicking-off in mid-afternoon.

KUWAIT

Colours: blue shirts, blue shorts (*reserve colours:* red shirts, white shorts)

Dark horses: Kuwait, the minnows in Group Four with England, Czechoslovakia and France.

For all of Saudi Arabia's investments in football through facilities and the importing of many English and other experts, Kuwait finished as leaders of the Asia-

Oceania group. Saudi Arabia failed to win a match in the extraordinary final round. It is ironic that in the finals Kuwait are in England's group.

Kuwait could then sit back and watch New Zealand and China struggle right into World Cup year itself for the last of all the 24 places in Spain. They had won four of their games in the last round and lost only to the rapidly developing Chinese (3-0). Their achievement was remarkable for a country with just 1,638 registered players in a population of one million and a Football Association only 30 years old. They were well rewarded for investing in a Brazilian coach, Carlos Alberto Parreira (not Brazil's 1970 World Cup captain of the same name).

An advantage was given when it was decided to hold all of the early group qualifying matches, also involving South Korea, Malaysia and Thailand, in Kuwait. Iran withdrew when football in that country

was abandoned, leaving Kuwait to win all three matches and not concede a single goal. They overwhelmed Thailand 6-0, beat Malaysia 4-0 and South Korea 1-0.

The South Koreans, backed by experience from several foreign tours, were disappointing. Kuwait had beaten them in the Asian Cup Final. For the World Cup qualifiers, Alberto built on the basis of a side established by his predecessor, Mario Zagalo, once manager of Brazil.

Promising a lively series of games in the final round, the president of the Kuwait Football Association, Sheik Fahad Al Sabah, said after seeing New Zealand and China draw 0-0 that if the New Zealanders played as roughly against his team 'we will be rougher'. The side chosen to play in Auckland included many of the players who had reached the quarter-finals of the Olympic competition in Moscow. Sure enough the match was rough.

The New Zealand supporters were angered by the Indonesian referee who awarded 33 free-kicks and two penalties to

High jinks: Said al Hoti leaps above New Zealand's Steve Wooddin in October 1981.

Kuwait and only 10 free-kicks in favour of the home side. They pelted the linesmen with cans. A spectator ran on to the pitch and the match had to be stopped for 10 minutes. Then the New Zealand goalkeeper saved a penalty and his side took the lead, temporarily pacifying the record crowd of 35,000.

A second penalty, from which Faisal Al-Dakheel scored, again inflamed the crowd but Kuwait answered them by scoring the winning goal from a header by Yacoub.

Kuwait went to China full of confidence yet lost 3-0, partly because they failed to score from a penalty given when they were a goal down. China went straight back into the attack, scored two more goals and Kuwait did well to recover their composure in time to beat Saudi Arabia 1-0 in Riyadh.

The return game against China attracted 25,000 people and Kuwait's 1-0 victory compensated for the heavy away defeat. One of the Kuwait midfield players, Abdel-Aziz Alnbari, shot the winning goal from 30 yards. Two more goals from Al-Dakheel against Saudi Arabia assured Kuwait of a place in Spain but there they are likely to find that oil-money cannot buy experience. Nevertheless, Brazilian influence has brought Kuwait international recognition.

NEW ZEALAND

Colours: White shirts, black shorts (*reserve colours:* black shirts, white shorts)

New Zealand have travelled further (64,000 miles), scored more goals in a single game (13) and played more matches (15) than any other team going to Spain. They were the last to qualify and will be making their first appearance in the finals.

Their journey was eventful as well as long. The adventure came to a climax in Singapore where on a sultry day in January they beat China 2-1 in a special play-off match to join Kuwait as qualifiers from the Asia and Oceania Group. Less than a month before most people had written them off.

In their last play-off group match in Riyadh they had to beat Saudi Arabia by five clear goals to force China into a decider for Spain. A six-goal win seemed out of the question. Amazingly they took a 5-0 half-time lead. Wynton Rufer, a 19-year-old striker who later tried to join Norwich City in the English league, and Brian Turner scored two each. Tranmere reject, Steve Wooddin, got the fifth. This put them equal with China on points and goal difference. Surprisingly, they failed to score a single second-half goal.

Kuala Lumpur was the first choice for the play-off against China but New Zealand objected because the Chinese had played qualifying games there. The match was switched to Singapore where a 60,000 crowd, almost all roaring for China, saw Rufer have the game of his life. He made the first goal for New Zealand, pushing the ball across the edge of the penalty area for Wooddin to crack a left-foot drive into the far corner.

In the second half goalkeeper Wilson's clearance was headed on to Rufer who hammered the ball past China's goalkeeper Li Fusheng from 20 yards. The Chinese fought back and Huang Xiangdon sent a crashing drive into the roof of the net. But New Zealand sweeper Bobby Almond stood firm to ensure that Wu Yuhua's succession of centres came to nothing.

So a country of 900 million bowed to one of under three million. China had spent years in the football wilderness before and during the Cultural Revolution as a result of their objections to FIFA's recognition of Taiwan. Now their skilful but inexperienced team must wait for another chance

Wooddin is challenged by Naim Sa'ad (on the ground) and Abdula Mayouf during New Zealand's World Cup match in Auckland.

Last ticket to Spain

New Zealand clinched the final place in Spain by beating China 2-1 in a special play-off match in Singapore in January 1982. They earned this play-off with a dramatic 5-0 win over Saudi Arabia in Riyadh. (If they had won by six clear goals they would not have needed a play-off and they went 5-0 up before half-time but could not improve on this in the second half.) In Singapore they were meeting China for the third time, having achieved a goalless draw in Peking and a 1-0 victory at home. The illustration shows New Zealand's winning goal scored by 18-year-old Winton Rufer. He had the game of his life and later tried to join the English second division club, Norwich City. Rufer had made the first New Zealand goal for Wooddin who hit a left-foot shot from the edge of the penalty area. Ninety seconds into the second half New Zealand goalkeeper Richard Wilton pumped a long punt upfield. The ball was headed on to Rufer. The teenager collected the ball outside the penalty area, slipped past a despairing defensive tackle and coolly slotted the ball past Chinese goalkeeper Li Fusheng from 20 yards. This great goal was a fitting way for the 24th team to enter the finals. The Chinese did not give up without a fight and Huang Xiangdon narrowed the gap but could not equalize.

while New Zealand get an opportunity to show they can play soccer as well as rugby.

Before this World Cup Australia always had the edge over New Zealand. The Australians spent £400,000 on preparations but they lost at home to the Kiwis for the first time early in the qualifying group. The architect of New Zealand's 2-0 victory was their manager, former Exeter City and Hartlepool player John Adshead.

In eight group qualifying games New Zealand were unbeaten and scored 31 goals. They made Fiji suffer miserably. The Fijians lost 10-0 in Australia and arrived in New Zealand still suffering from hangovers after drowning their sorrows. They went down 13-0, a World Cup record defeat. New Zealand skipper Steve Sumner (ex-Preston North End) scored six times.

Having drawn 0-0 in Peking and beaten China 1-0 at home, New Zealand had the psychological advantage when they came face to face for a third time. Much as the Chinese impressed Adshead with their pace ('we knew they had two good wingers but nobody told us about the other nine') they lacked strength and height in attack. Not that it was easy for New Zealand in Singapore.

Based on players with English league experience, the New Zealand side has a sound defensive heart. Almond (ex-Orient and Tottenham Hotspur) and Herbert are powerful central defenders. Sumner is a leader in midfield and loves scoring goals. In attack Wooddin and Brian Turner have been highly successful, but usually against crumbling defences.

New Zealand's achievement is to be among the final 24. They are unlucky to be drawn in one of the toughest groups in the finals and will not expect a comfortable time in Spain, but Adshead has done well with limited resources: 'The whole thing was done on a shoestring – the players even had to take home their own kit for washing.'

Left: polished Kiwis: New Zealand is best known as a rugby nation and before this World Cup had always been second best to Australia on the soccer pitch but they earned their passage to Spain the hard way after 15 qualifying matches. The team which beat China in Auckland is (left to right): Herbert, Elrick, Cole, G. Turner, Dods, Almond, Mackay, McClure, B. Turner, Sumner and Wilson.

QUALIFYING RESULTS AND LEAGUE TABLES

EUROPE

GROUP ONE

Finland 0   Bulgaria 2
Albania 2   Finland 0
Finland 0   Austria 2
Bulgaria 2   Albania 1
Austria 5   Albania 0
Bulgaria 1   W. Germany 3
Albania 0   Austria 1
Albania 0   W. Germany 2
W. Germany 2   Austria 0
Bulgaria 4   Finland 0

Finland 0   W. Germany 4
Austria 2   Bulgaria 0
Austria 5   Finland 0
Finland 2   Albania 1
W. Germany 7   Finland 1
Austria 1   W. Germany 3
Albania 0   Bulgaria 2
Bulgaria 0   Austria 0
W. Germany 8   Albania 0
W. Germany 4   Bulgaria 0

	P	W	D	L	F	A	Pts
West Germany	8	8	0	0	33	3	16
Austria	8	5	1	2	16	6	11
Bulgaria	8	4	1	3	11	10	9
Albania	8	1	0	7	4	22	2
Finland	8	1	0	7	4	27	2

West Germany and Austria qualify for finals.

GROUP THREE

Iceland 0   Wales 4
Iceland 1   USSR 2
Turkey 1   Iceland 3
USSR 5   Iceland 0
Wales 4   Turkey 0
Wales 1   Czechoslovakia 0
Czechoslovakia 2   Turkey 0
Turkey 0   Wales 1
Turkey 0   Czechoslovakia 3
Czechoslovakia 6   Iceland 1

Wales 0   USSR 0
Iceland 2   Turkey 0
Czechoslovakia 2   Wales 0
USSR 4   Turkey 0
Iceland 1   Czechoslovakia 1
Turkey 0   USSR 3
Wales 2   Iceland 2
USSR 2   Czechoslovakia 0
USSR 3   Wales 0
Czechoslovakia 1   USSR 1

	P	W	D	L	F	A	Pts
USSR	8	6	2	0	20	2	14
Czechoslovakia	8	4	2	2	15	6	10
Wales	8	4	2	2	12	7	10
Iceland	8	2	2	4	10	21	6
Turkey	8	0	0	8	1	22	0

USSR and Czechoslovakia qualify for finals.

GROUP TWO

Cyprus 2   Rep. of Ireland 3
Rep. of Ireland 2   Holland 1
Cyprus 0   France 7
Rep. of Ireland 1   Belgium 1
France 2   Rep. of Ireland 0
Belgium 1   Holland 0
Rep. of Ireland 6   Cyprus 0
Cyprus 0   Belgium 2
Belgium 3   Cyprus 2
Holland 3   Cyprus 0

Holland 1   France 0
Belgium 1   Rep. of Ireland 0
France 3   Belgium 2
Cyprus 0   Holland 1
Holland 2   Rep. of Ireland 2
Belgium 2   France 0
Holland 3   Belgium 0
Rep. of Ireland 3   France 2
France 2   Holland 0
France 4   Cyprus 0

	P	W	D	L	F	A	Pts
Belgium	8	5	1	2	12	9	11
France	8	5	0	3	20	8	10
Republic of Ireland	8	4	2	2	17	11	10
Holland	8	4	1	3	11	7	9
Cyprus	8	0	0	8	4	29	0

Belgium and France qualify for finals.

GROUP FOUR

England 4   Norway 0
Norway 1   Romania 1
Romania 2   England 1
Switzerland 1   Norway 2
England 2   Switzerland 1
England 0   Romania 0
Switzerland 2   Hungary 2
Hungary 1   Romania 0
Norway 1   Hungary 2
Switzerland 2   England 1

Romania 1   Norway 0
Hungary 1   England 3
Norway 1   Switzerland 1
Norway 2   England 1
Romania 0   Hungary 0
Romania 1   Switzerland 2
Hungary 3   Switzerland 0
Hungary 4   Norway 1
Switzerland 0   Romania 0
England 1   Hungary 0

	P	W	D	L	F	A	Pts
Hungary	8	4	2	2	13	8	10
England	8	4	1	3	13	8	9
Romania	8	2	4	2	5	5	8
Switzerland	8	2	3	3	9	12	7
Norway	8	2	2	4	8	15	6

Hungary and England qualify for finals.

GROUP FIVE

Luxembourg 0   Yugoslavia 5   Luxembourg 1   Denmark 2
Yugoslavia 2   Denmark 1   Yugoslavia 5   Greece 1
Luxembourg 0   Italy 2   Denmark 3   Italy 1
Denmark 0   Greece 1   Denmark 1   Yugoslavia 2
Italy 2   Denmark 0   Greece 2   Denmark 3
Italy 2   Yugoslavia 0   Yugoslavia 1   Italy 1
Denmark 4   Luxembourg 0   Italy 1   Greece 1
Greece 0   Italy 2   Yugoslavia 5   Luxembourg 0
Greece 2   Luxembourg 0   Greece 1   Yugoslavia 2
Luxembourg 0   Greece 2   Italy 1   Luxembourg 0

	P	W	D	L	F	A	Pts
Yugoslavia	8	6	1	1	22	7	13
Italy	8	5	2	1	12	5	12
Denmark	8	4	0	4	14	11	8
Greece	8	3	1	4	10	13	7
Luxembourg	8	0	0	8	1	23	0

Yugoslavia and Italy qualify for finals.

GROUP SIX

Israel 0   N. Ireland 0   N. Ireland 1   Portugal 0
Sweden 1   Israel 1   Scotland 3   Israel 1
Sweden 0   Scotland 1   Sweden 1   N. Ireland 0
N. Ireland 3   Sweden 0   Sweden 3   Portugal 0
Scotland 0   Portugal 0   Scotland 2   Sweden 0
Israel 0   Sweden 0   Portugal 1   Sweden 2
Portugal 1   N. Ireland 0   N. Ireland 0   Scotland 0
Portugal 3   Israel 0   Israel 4   Portugal 1
Israel 0   Scotland 1   N. Ireland 1   Israel 0
Scotland 1   N. Ireland 1   Portugal 2   Scotland 1

	P	W	D	L	F	A	Pts
Scotland	8	4	3	1	9	4	11
Northern Ireland	8	3	3	2	6	3	9
Sweden	8	3	2	3	7	8	8
Portugal	8	3	1	4	8	11	7
Israel	8	1	3	4	6	10	5

Scotland and Northern Ireland qualify for finals.

GROUP SEVEN

Malta 0   Poland 2 (abandoned)   E. Germany 2   Poland 3
Malta 1   E. Germany 2   E. Germany 5   Malta 1
Poland 1   E. Germany 0   Poland 6   Malta 0

	P	W	D	L	F	A	Pts
Poland	4	4	0	0	12	2	8
East Germany	4	2	0	2	9	6	4
Malta	4	0	0	4	2	15	0

Poland qualify for finals.

SOUTH AMERICA

GROUP ONE

Venezuela 0   Brazil 1   Venezuela 1   Bolivia 0
Bolivia 3   Venezuela 0   Brazil 3   Bolivia 1
Bolivia 1   Brazil 2   Brazil 5   Venezuela 0

	P	W	D	L	F	A	Pts
Brazil	4	4	0	0	11	2	8
Bolivia	4	1	0	3	5	6	2
Venezuela	4	1	0	3	1	9	2

Brazil qualify for finals.

GROUP TWO

Colombia 1   Peru 1   Uruguay 1   Peru 2
Uruguay 3   Colombia 2   Peru 0   Uruguay 0
Peru 2   Colombia 0   Colombia 1   Uruguay 1

	P	W	D	L	F	A	Pts
Peru	4	2	2	0	5	2	6
Uruguay	4	1	2	1	5	5	4
Colombia	4	0	2	2	4	7	2

Peru qualify for finals.

GROUP THREE

Ecuador 1   Paraguay 0   Paraguay 0   Chile 1
Ecuador 0   Chile 0   Chile 2   Ecuador 0
Paraguay 3   Ecuador 1   Chile 3   Paraguay 0

	P	W	D	L	F	A	Pts
Chile	4	3	1	0	6	0	7
Ecuador	4	1	1	2	2	5	3
Paraguay	4	1	0	3	3	6	2

Chile qualify for finals.

SOUTH AND CENTRAL AMERICA

NORTHERN ZONE

Canada 1   Mexico 1
United States 0   Canada 0
Canada 2   United States 1

Mexico 5   United States 1
Mexico 1   Canada 1
United States 2   Mexico 1

	P	W	D	L	F	A	Pts
Canada	4	1	3	0	4	3	5
Mexico	4	1	2	1	8	5	4
United States	4	1	1	2	4	8	3

Canada and Mexico qualified for final CONCACAF games.

CENTRAL ZONE

Panama 0   Guatemala 2
Panama 0   Honduras 2
Panama 1   Costa Rica 1
Panama 1   El Salvador 3
Costa Rica 2   Honduras 3
El Salvador 4   Panama 1
Guatemala 0   Costa Rica 0
Honduras 2   El Salvador 0
Honduras 0   Guatemala 0
El Salvador 2   Costa Rica 0

Costa Rica 2   Panama 0
Guatemala 0   El Salvador 0
Guatemala 5   Panama 0
Honduras 1   Costa Rica 1
El Salvador 2   Honduras 1
Costa Rica 0   Guatemala 3
Guatemala 0   Honduras 1
Costa Rica 0   El Salvador 0
Honduras 5   Panama 0
El Salvador 1   Guatemala 0

	P	W	D	L	F	A	Pts
Honduras	8	5	2	1	15	5	12
El Salvador	8	5	2	1	12	5	12
Guatemala	8	3	3	2	10	2	9
Costa Rica	8	1	4	3	6	10	6
Panama	8	0	1	7	3	24	1

Honduras and El Salvador qualified for final CONCACAF games.

CARIBBEANS

SUB GROUP A
Guyana 5   Grenada 2
(Guyana qualified for Group A)

Grenada 2   Guyana 3

GROUP A
Cuba 3   Surinam 0
Surinam 0   Cuba 0
Guyana 0   Surinam 1

Surinam 4   Guyana 0
Cuba 1   Guyana 0
Guyana 0   Cuba 3

	P	W	D	L	F	A	Pts
Cuba	4	3	1	0	7	0	7
Surinam	4	2	1	1	5	3	5
Guyana	4	0	0	4	0	9	0

Cuba qualified for final CONCACAF games.

GROUP B
Haiti 2   Trinidad and Tobago 0
Trinidad and Tobago 1   Haiti 0
Netherlands Antilles 1   Haiti 1
Haiti 1   Netherlands Antilles 0
Trinidad and Tobago 0   Netherlands Antilles 0
Netherlands Antilles 0   Trinidad and Tobago 0

	P	W	D	L	F	A	Pts
Haiti	4	2	1	1	4	2	5
Trinidad and Tobago	4	1	2	1	1	2	4
Netherlands Antilles	4	0	3	1	1	2	3

Haiti qualified for final CONCACAF games.

FINAL CONCACAF GAMES

Mexico 4   Cuba 0
Canada 1   El Salvador 0
Honduras 4   Haiti 0
Haiti 1   Canada 1
Mexico 0   El Salvador 1
Honduras 2   Cuba 0
El Salvador 0   Cuba 0
Mexico 1   Haiti 1

Honduras 2   Canada 1
Haiti 0   Cuba 2
Mexico 1   Canada 1
Honduras 0   El Salvador 0
Haiti 0   El Salvador 1
Cuba 2   Canada 2
Honduras 0   Mexico 0

	P	W	D	L	F	A	Pts
Honduras	5	3	2	0	8	1	8
El Salvador	5	2	2	1	2	1	6
Mexico	5	1	3	1	6	3	5
Canada	5	1	3	1	6	6	5
Cuba	5	1	2	2	4	8	4
Haiti	5	0	2	3	2	9	2

Honduras and El Salvador qualify for finals.

AFRICA

FIRST ROUND

FIRST GAMES:

Libya 2   Gambia 1
Ethiopia 0   Zambia 0
Sierra Leone 2   Algeria 2
Tunisia 2   Nigeria 0
Senegal 0   Morocco 1

Zaire 5   Mozambique 2
Cameroon 3   Malawi 0
Guinea 3   Lesotho 1
Niger 0   Somalia 0
Kenya 3   Tanzania 1

Ghana and Uganda withdrew
Madagascar and Egypt walked over.

SECOND GAMES:

Gambia 0   Libya 0 (Libya won 1-2 on aggregate)
Zambia 4   Ethiopia 0 (4-0)
Algeria 3   Sierra Leone 1 (5-3)
Nigeria 2   Tunisia 0 (2-2, 4-3 on penalty kicks)
Morocco 0   Senegal 0 (1-0)
Mozambique 1   Zaire 2 (3-7)
Malawi 1   Cameroon 1 (1-4)
Lesotho 1   Guinea 1 (2-4)
Somalia 0   Niger 1 (0-1)
Tanzania 5   Kenya 0 (6-3)

SECOND ROUND

FIRST GAMES:

(Zimbabwe, Sudan, Liberia, Togo classified directly to this round)
Algeria 2   Sudan 0
Niger 0   Togo 1
Liberia 0   Guinea 0
Cameroon 2   Zimbabwe 0
Morocco 2   Zambia 0
Nigeria 1   Tanzania 1
Madagascar 1   Zaire 1

SECOND GAMES:

Sudan 1   Algeria 1 (1-3)
Togo 1   Niger 2 (2-2, Niger won on away goals)
Guinea 1   Liberia 0 (1-0)
Zimbabwe 1   Cameroon 0 (1-2)
Zambia 2   Morocco 0 (2-2, Morocco won 5-4 on penalty kicks)
Tanzania 0   Nigeria 2 (1-3)
Zaire 3   Madagascar 2 (4-3)
Libya withdrew. Egypt walked over.

THIRD ROUND

FIRST GAMES:

Algeria 4   Niger 0
Guinea 1   Nigeria 1
Morocco 1   Egypt 0
Zaire 1   Cameroon 0

SECOND GAMES:

Niger 1   Algeria 0 (1-4)
Nigeria 1   Guinea 0 (2-1)
Egypt 0   Morocco 0 (0-1)
Cameroon 6   Zaire 1 (6-2)

FOURTH ROUND

FIRST GAMES:
Nigeria 0   Algeria 2
Morocco 0   Cameroon 2

SECOND GAMES:
Algeria 2   Nigeria 1 (4-1)
Cameroon 2   Morocco 1 (4-1)

Algeria and Cameroon qualified for finals.

ASIA AND OCEANIA

GROUP ONE

Indonesia 1   Australia 0
Indonesia 3   Fiji Island 3
Indonesia 0   New Zealand 2
Indonesia 1   Taiwan 0
Australia 2   Indonesia 0
Australia 10   Fiji 0
Australia 0   New Zealand 2
Australia 3   Taiwan 2
Fiji 0   Indonesia 0
Fiji 1   Australia 4

Fiji 0   New Zealand 4
Fiji 2   Taiwan 1
New Zealand 5   Indonesia 0
New Zealand 3   Australia 3
New Zealand 13   Fiji 0
New Zealand 2   Taiwan 0
Taiwan 2   Indonesia 0
Taiwan 0   Australia 0
Taiwan 0   Fiji 0
Taiwan 0   New Zealand 0

	P	W	D	L	F	A	Pts
New Zealand	8	6	2	0	31	3	14
Australia	8	4	2	2	22	9	10
Indonesia	8	2	2	4	5	14	6
Taiwan	8	1	3	4	5	8	5
Fiji	8	1	3	4	6	35	5

New Zealand qualified for final Asia and Oceania round.

GROUP TWO

Iraq 2   Syria 1
Iraq 2   Bahrain 0
Iraq 0   Saudi Arabia 1
Syria 0   Bahrain 1
Syria 0   Saudi Arabia 2

Bahrain 0   Saudi Arabia 1
Qatar 0   Iraq 1
Qatar 2   Syria 1
Qatar 3   Bahrain 0
Qatar 0   Saudi Arabia 1

	P	W	D	L	F	A	Pts
Saudi Arabia	4	4	0	0	5	0	8
Iraq	4	3	0	1	5	2	6
Qatar	4	2	0	2	5	3	4
Bahrain	4	1	0	3	1	6	2
Syria	4	0	0	4	2	7	0

Saudi Arabia qualified for final Asia and Oceania round.

GROUP THREE

Kuwait 6	Thailand 0			Thailand 2	Malaysia 2		
Kuwait 4	Malaysia 0			Thailand 1	South Korea 5		
Kuwait 2	South Korea 0			Malaysia 1	South Korea 2		

Iran withdrew.

	P	W	D	L	F	A	Pts
Kuwait	3	3	0	0	12	0	6
South Korea	3	2	0	1	7	4	4
Malaysia	3	0	1	2	3	8	1
Thailand	3	0	1	2	3	13	1

Kuwait qualified for final Asia and Oceania round.

GROUP FOUR

PRELIMINARY ROUND:

GROUP A

Hong Kong 0	China 1	China 3	Macao 0
Japan 1	Singapore 0	China 1	Japan 0
North Korea 3	Macao 0	Japan 3	Macao 0

	P	W	D	L	F	A	Pts
China	2	2	0	0	4	0	4
Japan	2	1	0	1	3	1	2
Macao	2	0	0	2	0	6	0

GROUP B

North Korea 1	Singapore 0
Singapore 1	Hong Kong 1
North Korea 2	Hong Kong 2

	P	W	D	L	F	A	Pts
North Korea	2	1	1	0	3	2	3
Hong Kong	2	0	2	0	3	3	2
Singapore	2	0	1	1	1	2	1

SEMI-FINAL ROUND
North Korea 1   Japan 0
China 0   Hong Kong 0
(China won 5-4 on penalty kicks.)

FINAL
China 4   North Korea 2 (aet)
China qualified for final Asia and Oceania round.

FINAL ROUND

China 0	New Zealand 0	Saudi Arabia 0	Kuwait 1
New Zealand 1	China 0	Saudi Arabia 2	China 4
New Zealand 1	Kuwait 2	China 2	Saudi Arabia 0
China 3	Kuwait 0	New Zealand 2	Saudi Arabia 2

Kuwait 1	China 0	Kuwait 2	New Zealand 2
Kuwait 2	Saudi Arabia 0	Saudi Arabia 0	New Zealand 5

	P	W	D	L	F	A	Pts
Kuwait	6	4	1	1	8	6	9
China	6	3	1	2	9	4	7
New Zealand	6	2	3	1	11	6	7
Saudi Arabia	6	0	1	5	4	16	1

Play-off: New Zealand 2   China 1.
Kuwait and New Zealand qualify for finals.

Records from 11 previous final competitions (only of those who have qualified for Spain)

	P	W	D	L	F	A
Brazil	52	33	10	9	119	56
West Germany	47	28	9	10	110	68
Italy	36	20	6	10	62	40
Argentina	29	14	5	10	55	43
Hungary	26	13	2	11	73	42
England	24	10	6	8	34	28
Yugoslavia	25	10	5	10	45	34
USSR	19	10	3	6	30	21
Poland	14	9	1	4	27	17
Austria	18	9	1	8	33	36
Czechoslovakia	22	8	3	11	32	36
France	20	8	1	11	43	38
Chile	18	7	3	8	23	24
Spain	18	7	3	8	22	25
Peru	12	4	1	7	17	25
Scotland	11	2	4	5	12	21
Northern Ireland	5	2	1	2	6	10
Belgium	9	1	1	7	12	25
El Salvador	3	0	0	3	0	9

Algeria, Honduras, Cameroon, Kuwait and New Zealand have no previous experience of finals.

The draw in the Exhibition and Congress Palace, Madrid, on 16 January 1982 was an unhappy business for the organizers. France and Belgium had already complained that England had been seeded among the top six. Their objections rumbled on but were overruled.

In an attempt to make the draw as well balanced as possible, the 24 qualifiers were ranked in four groups of six seeds. The six first-phase groups were to have one team from each tier of seeds. After the top six (Italy, West Germany, Argentina, England, Spain and Brazil) came the second tier of seeds: Austria and the five East European qualifiers, Czechoslovakia, Hungary, Poland, the Soviet Union and Yugoslavia.

France and Belgium were among the third-ranked seeds with Scotland, Northern Ireland, Chile and Peru. Ironically, if Holland had qualified, England would have dropped from the first to the third tier of seeds. In the fourth tier were the six minnows: Algeria, Cameroon, El Salvador, Honduras, Kuwait and New Zealand.

The top seeds were placed at the head of their respective groups. With the names of the remaining finalists concealed in little footballs, there was a draw to decide on the order of the groups of seeds.

The little footballs were spun in wire cages used for the Spanish lottery. The third-ranked nations were drawn first and Belgium were the first to appear. That meant they were destined to meet Argentina in the opening match of the tournament but they were mistakenly put in Group One with Italy. Confusion reigned.

The stage is set: the draw for the 1982 finals as it happened in the magnificent Exhibition and Congress Palace, Madrid, on 16 January 1982.

For a fleeting moment Scotland were set to play the inaugural match against the holders. But the slip was spotted. The ceremony went ahead with a few more hitches but, finally, the draw was concluded. It revealed some fascinating combinations.

Group One
Italy and Poland are favourites to go through to the second phase. Their meeting in Vigo on the second day of the finals should be an early highlight. Poland eliminated Italy in the first stage of the 1974 finals, having already put out England in the qualifying competition. In 1974 Italy lost 2-1, needing only a draw to move forward and Argentina qualified for the second phase on goal difference.

Peru burst Scotland's bubble in 1978 and they will hope to punish any weaknesses in the top two. Italy have the third best record in the finals, but they have also suffered disasters, such as dismal failure in 1966. Poland were third in 1974 but they will need iron in their souls to forget the poli-

Above: the World Cup organizing committee and (*right*): the moment of truth: a ball containing a country's name in the draw is handed to Hermann Neuberger, the West German delegate. Some technical hitches prevented the proceedings from going smoothly.

tical crisis at home. Cameroon will make up the numbers.

Group Two
West Germany have been given the chance of taking revenge on Austria, who beat them 3-2 in the second phase in 1978. Both can reach the next round again at the expense of Chile and Algeria. But Chile may throw Austria's dreams to the high sierras when their teams meet on 17 June.

Group Three
Argentina and Belgium kick off the 12th World Cup finals hoping to end the run of four goalless draws. But Belgium's solid teamwork may prolong the sequence. These two should qualify for the second stage ahead of Hungary and El Salvador. Watch out for fireworks at Elche when

116

Argentina and Hungary clash. In the 1978 finals these two met in the early phase and two Hungarians were sent off.

Group Four
England had the kindest draw of the three British contenders. Their first outing in Bilbao is against the skilful French on 16 June. Then they play Czechoslovakia on 20 June. The Czechs won the 1976 European championships, removing England in the pre-qualifying round. But they have won only twice and drawn twice in nine matches against England. Czechoslovakia lost 1-0 to England in the 1970 finals.

France's record against England is worse. Their best result was a 5-2 win in 1963 in England's first game under the command of Alf Ramsey. This insult was readily repaid with England's 2-0 victory in the 1966 World Cup finals and a 5-0 drubbing of France at Wembley in 1969. England's last match in the group will be against Kuwait, who are managed by the Brazilian Carlos Alberto.

Group Five
Spain could be surprised by Northern Ireland who are dangerous because they have nothing to lose. Irish eyes will be smiling if they achieve a good result in their first match, against Yugoslavia on 17 June. The last group game between Spain and Northern Ireland in Valencia on 25 June could be tense. Irish manager Billy Bingham hopes that Spain will have qualified already for the next phase and so the pressure will be less intense.

Group Six
A cruel draw for Scotland has paired them with the favourites, Brazil, and the most fancied outsiders, the Soviet Union, two nations they have never beaten. Gritty New Zealand will provide no practice match for the Scots in their first game. The Scots did hold Brazil to a 0-0 draw in the 1974 finals.

'It could not have been harder,' Scotland's manager Jock Stein said. 'I think we are drawn with two teams who could play

117

in the final itself. The Russians are on the verge of something special.'

Unluckily for Scotland their first match is against New Zealand in Malaga on 15 June. The Kiwis will be all fired up to prove that a rugby-mad nation is worthy of a place in soccer's big pool. The game between Brazil and the Soviet Union on 14 June could provide something to savour. Scotland will have done well if they are not on the first flight home after their game against the Soviet Union on 22 June.

The first two nations in these six groups will advance to the second phase of four groups of three teams. If the seedings work out, there would be some shape to Groups A, B, C and D. But nothing is certain, least of all in soccer although the first round will provide a form guide.

The chart that follows shows how the qualifiers for the second phase will be regrouped. The winners of these four groups go forward to the semi-finals.

The organizers originally planned a set fixture list for the second phase, which runs from 28 June to 5 July. But they soon realized that they had to make the system more flexible. By winning the first two matches in the second phase, a team would qualify for the semi-finals and kill interest in the third game.

Now the team which *loses* the first match in the second phase will play the remaining member of the group. Whatever happens, there will be everything to play for in the third second-phase matches.

Group A may include Italy (as winners of Group One), Argentina (winners of Group Three) and Scotland or the Soviet Union (runners-up in Group Six). Unless Italy find a rich vein of form, the unseeded nation could pose a greater threat to Argentina. But the holders may carry their defence of the World Cup to the semi-finals.

Group B should fall to West Germany (as

winners of Group Two). England will be in this group if they win Group Four, together with Yugoslavia or possibly Northern Ireland (runners-up in Group Five). Perhaps England would do better to finish as runners-up in Group Four and avoid West Germany in the second phase. In that case they could face Spain in Group D, not an easy proposition in Madrid.

Group C should be tailor-made for Brazil (winners of Group Six). Poland (runners-up in Group One) and Belgium (runners-up in Group Three) are their likely opponents.

Group D seems certain to be the most hotly contested in the second phase, with Austria or Chile (runners-up in Group Two), France (runners-up in Group Four) and Spain (winners in Group Five) the possible contenders.

The semi-finals on 8 July could be Argentina v Brazil (winners of Group A v winners of Group C) in the Nou Camp Stadium, Barcelona, and West Germany v Spain (winners of Group B v winners of Group D) in Seville. The losing semi-finalists play off for third place in Alicante on 10 July.

The winners meet in the Bernabeu Stadium, Madrid, the following day and form points to a marvellous Brazil v West Germany final. Sentiment suggests that erratic England will somehow find their way past West Germany in the second phase and Spain in the semi-finals to contest the final with Brazil. If Brazil stick to their natural style they have a favourite's chance of winning the World Cup for the fourth time.

FORMAT FOR THE FINALS

The chart that follows shows how the draw worked out and provides the dates and venues for each match.

In the first round (pages 121 to 123) the 24 nations have been split into six groups (One to Six) of four. These four play each other on a league basis and the first two in each group go forward to the second phase. If teams finish level on points the one with the better goal difference qualifies.

The format for the second phase is also laid out in advance. Countries can plot their paths and see who their likely opponents will be, whether they finish first or second in their group.

The 12 teams that qualify from the first round are regrouped into four groups of three (A, B, C and D) and the winners of each of these leagues go through to the semi-finals which are played on a knockout basis. The losing semi-finalists play off for third place. The winning semi-finalists meet in the final which will be held in the Bernabeu Stadium, Madrid.

GROUP ONE

	P	W	D	L	F	A	Pts
	3						
	3						
	3						
	3						

Winner to Group A

Runner-up to Group C

ITALY	0	POLAND	0	14 JUNE	BALAIDOS
PERU		CAMEROON		15 JUNE	RIAZOR
ITALY	1	PERU	1	18 JUNE	BALAIDOS
POLAND	0	CAMEROON	0	19 JUNE	RIAZOR
PERU	1	POLAND	5	22 JUNE	RIAZOR
ITALY		CAMEROON		23 JUNE	BALAIDOS

GROUP TWO

	P	W	D	L	F	A	Pts
	3						
	3						
	3						
	3						

Winner to Group B

Runner-up to Group D

WEST GERMANY	1	ALGERIA	2	16 JUNE	EL MOLINON
CHILE	0	AUSTRIA	1	17 JUNE	CARLOS TARTIERE
WEST GERMANY	4	CHILE	1	20 JUNE	EL MOLINON
ALGERIA		AUSTRIA		21 JUNE	CARLOS TARTIERE
ALGERIA		CHILE		24 JUNE	CARLOS TARTIERE
WEST GERMANY		AUSTRIA		25 JUNE	EL MOLINON

GROUP THREE

	P	W	D	L	F	A	Pts
	3						
	3						
	3						
	3						

Winner to Group A

Runner-up to Group C

ARGENTINA	0	BELGIUM	1	13 JUNE	JOSE RICO PEREZ
HUNGARY	10	EL SALVADOR	1	15 JUNE	NUEVO ESTADIO
ARGENTINA	4	HUNGARY	1	18 JUNE	JOSE RICO PEREZ
BELGIUM	3	EL SALVADOR	1	19 JUNE	NUEVO ESTADIO
BELGIUM	1	HUNGARY	1	22 JUNE	NUEVO ESTADIO
ARGENTINA		EL SALVADOR		23 JUNE	JOSE RICO PEREZ

GROUP FOUR

	P	W	D	L	F	A	Pts
	3						
	3						
	3						
	3						

Winner to Group B

Runner-up to Group D

ENGLAND	3	FRANCE	1	16 JUNE	SAN MAMES
CZECHOSLOVAKIA	2	KUWAIT	1	17 JUNE	EL PRADO
ENGLAND	2	CZECHOSLOVAKIA	0	20 JUNE	SAN MAMES
FRANCE	4	KUWAIT	1	21 JUNE	EL PRADO
FRANCE		CZECHOSLOVAKIA		24 JUNE	EL PRADO
ENGLAND	1	KUWAIT	0	25 JUNE	SAN MAMES

GROUP FIVE

	P	W	D	L	F	A	Pts
	3						
	3						
	3						
	3						

Winner to Group D

Runner-up to Group B

SPAIN	1	HONDURAS	1	16 JUNE	LUIS CASANOVA
YUGOSLAVIA	0	NORTHERN IRELAND	0	17 JUNE	LA ROMAREDA
SPAIN		YUGOSLAVIA		20 JUNE	LUIS CASANOVA
HONDURAS	1	NORTHERN IRELAND	1	21 JUNE	LA ROMAREDA
HONDURAS		YUGOSLAVIA		24 JUNE	LA ROMAREDA
SPAIN	0	NORTHERN IRELAND	1	25 JUNE	LUIS CASANOVA

GROUP SIX

	P	W	D	L	F	A	Pts
	3						
	3						
	3						
	3						

Winner to Group C

Runner-up to Group A

BRAZIL	2	USSR	1	14 JUNE	VILLAMARIN SANCHEZ PIZJUAN
SCOTLAND	5	NEW ZEALAND	2	15 JUNE	LA ROSALEDA
BRAZIL	4	SCOTLAND	1	18 JUNE	VILLAMARIN SANCHEZ PIZJUAN
USSR	3	NEW ZEALAND	0	19 JUNE	LA ROSALEDA
USSR	2	SCOTLAND	2	22 JUNE	LA ROSALEDA
BRAZIL		NEW ZEALAND		23 JUNE	VILLAMARIN SANCHEZ PIZJUAN

SECOND ROUND

GROUP A

	P	W	D	L	F	A	Pts
	2						
	2						
	2						

Winner goes through to Semi-Finals (A)

				28 JUNE	NOU CAMP
				1 JULY	NOU CAMP
				4 JULY	NOU CAMP

GROUP B

	P	W	D	L	F	A	Pts
	2						
	2						
	2						

Winner goes through to Semi-Finals (B)

				29 JUNE	SANTIAGO BERNABEU
				2 JULY	SANTIAGO BERNABEU
				5 JULY	SANTIAGO BERNABEU

SEMI-FINALS

A		C		8 JULY	NOU CAMP

GROUP C

	P	W	D	L	F	A	Pts
	2						
	2						
	2						

**Winner goes through to
Semi-Finals (C)**

			29 JUNE	R.C.D. ESPAÑOL
			2 JULY	R.C.D. ESPAÑOL
			5 JULY	R.C.D. ESPAÑOL

GROUP D

	P	W	D	L	F	A	Pts
	2						
	2						
	2						

**Winner goes through to
Semi-Finals (D)**

			28 JUNE	VICENTE CALDERON
			1 JULY	VICENTE CALDERON
			4 JULY	VICENTE CALDERON

B		D		8 JULY	SANCHEZ PIZJUAN

THIRD PLACE MATCH

HALF-TIME

PLAYERS

_____

_____

_____

_____

_____

_____

_____

_____

_____

_____

_____

SUBSTITUTES

_____

MANAGER

_____

SCORERS

_____

_____

_____

_____

PLAYERS

_____

_____

_____

_____

_____

_____

_____

_____

_____

_____

_____

SUBSTITUTES

_____

MANAGER

_____

SCORERS

_____

_____

_____

_____

REFEREE

_____

LINESMEN

_____

_____

VENUE

_____

_____

ATTENDANCE

_____

DATE

_____

FINAL

| Italy | 3 | W. Germany | 1 | HALF-TIME | | |

PLAYERS

PLAYERS

REFEREE

LINESMEN

VENUE

ATTENDANCE

SUBSTITUTES

SUBSTITUTES

DATE

MANAGER

MANAGER

SCORERS

Rossi

SCORERS

ACKNOWLEDGMENTS

Front cover: Qualifying match between France and Belgium played at the Heysel Stadium, Brussels, on 9 September 1981. Photo: Peter Robinson

Back cover: 'Vigo' by Jacques Monory, one of a series of posters dedicated to the venues that will host the games of the World Cup. Photo: Central Press, London

The photographs in the historical section were supplied by Central Press, Keystone Press, Syndication International.
The photograph on page 40 was supplied by the Spanish Tourist Office, London.
The map on page 39 was drawn by Eugene Fleury.
Illustrations on pages 18, 21, 52, 74, 108-9, are by Bob Williams.